coffee cakes

# coffee cakes

○ ○ ○

simple, sweet, and savory

by *Lou Seibert Pappas*

○ ○ ○

photographs by *Maren Caruso*

CHRONICLE BOOKS
SAN FRANCISCO

Library of Congress Cataloging-in-Publication Data:
Pappas, Lou Seibert.
  Coffee cakes : simple, sweet, and savory / by Lou Seibert Pappas ;
photographs by Maren Caruso.
     p. cm.
  Includes index.
  ISBN-10: 0-8118-5507-4 (pb)
  ISBN-13: 978-0-8118-5507-5 (pb)
  1.  Coffee cakes.  I. Title.
  TX771.P343 2006
  641.8'659–dc22

                        2005031781


Manufactured in China.

Designed by Madeleine Budnick
Food and prop styling by Kim Konecny and Erin Quon
Assistant photography by Faiza Ali
Assistant food styling by Nicole Heather Slaven

Distributed in Canada by Raincoast Books
9050 Shaughnessy Street
Vancouver, British Columbia  V6P 6E5

10 9 8 7 6 5 4 3 2 1

Chronicle Books LLC
85 Second Street
San Francisco, California 94105

www.chroniclebooks.com

Bundt is a registered trademark of Northland Aluminum Products, Inc., Guittard is a registered trademark of
Guittard Chocolate Company, Hobart is a registered trademark of Premark FEG Corporation, RyKrisp is a registered
trademark of Ralston Purina Company, Sharffen Berger is a registered trademark of SVS Chocolate LLC.

## ACKNOWLEDGMENTS

Sharing the table with any one of the four accomplished Stewart sisters—Sandy, Claire, Sharon, and Kim—and their talented sister-in-law, Paula, is always an inspiration and delight, whether at their homes or dining out. My thanks to them for their love and support.

# table of contents

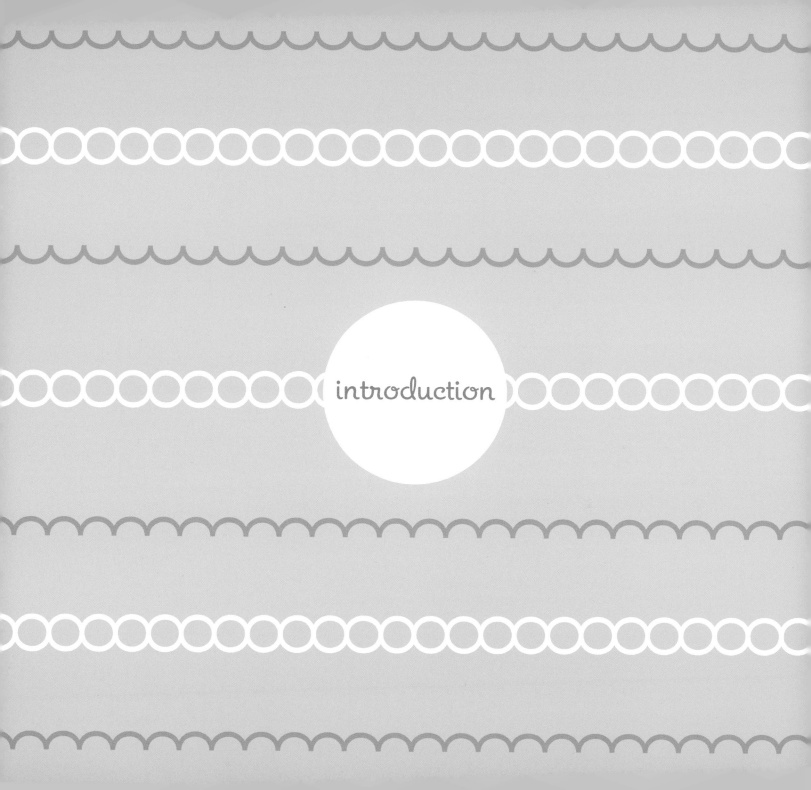

introduction

**F**ORTUITOUSLY, A TRIP TO SWEDEN to pursue my Scandinavian heritage was in the offing when I embarked on this cookbook. I wanted to visit Gothenburg, where my Swedish great-grandparents had a bakery at the end of the nineteenth century. Though the location of their ancient shop eluded me, every *bageri* tempted with delicious coffee cakes and tea rings galore, and my repertoire expanded as I darted into every bakery en route.

In an ancient square of Stockholm, I sipped hot chocolate from a huge stoneware soup bowl and munched a cinnamon pinwheel, an ambrosial match that prompted re-creating. On the enchanting island of Gotland, an elegantly restored thirteenth-century hotel offered cakes that were in vogue decades ago, proving that these treats are an enduring pleasure.

For centuries, coffee cakes have been a delicious adjunct to daily dining. Today, when coffee and chocolate drinks are an essential part of morning and afternoon rituals, scrumptious just-baked batter or yeast cakes are complementary companions.

My joy and passion for baking coffee cakes goes back to childhood. When I was growing up in Oregon, Swedish yeast breads, sticky caramel buns, and hazelnut-laced rings were everyday breakfast fare. Chocolate marble cakes, banana loaves, gingerbread, and apple, huckleberry, or prune plum coffee cakes were luscious sweets that filled the sideboard for coffee time and dessert. Mother had a commercial Hobart mixer that turned out batters and doughs with speed. And Grandma Helgesson produced her versions of these sweets on every visit.

Later, dozens of international trips introduced other ethnic cakes, both sweet and savory, that I re-created for family dining. Blessed with a dozen kinds of fruit trees and a wide choice of herbs, including lavender, my northern California garden supplies seasonal bounty. My fluted copper Bundt molds, carried back from France in the sixties, bake cakes to perfection.

The quintessential coffee cake—a streusel-topped butter cake—is thought to be an American creation. During the 1950s, "come for coffee" was an invitation among circles of housewives to sample this buttery cake or perhaps a gingerbread loaf, a peach torte, or a luscious blueberry Bundt cake. As American coffeehouses came into vogue, display cases were filled with glamorous pound cakes, marble cakes, and streusel cakes on pedestal plates under glass domes. Today, bakery cafés tantalize with coffee cakes and yeasted sweet breads. Our passion for Mediterranean fare has spurred a special fondness for French and Italian breads and cakes, such as brioche, focaccia, and polenta cake, and a variety of global bakery treats have joined American classics on bakery shelves.

The coffee-break tradition evolved from our forebears. The early days of the eighteenth century introduced coffee, tea, and chocolate drinks to the upper classes of Europe, and baked goods were a natural companion. Austrian and German coffeehouses, British high teas, and Scandinavian bakeries all featured sumptuous cakes and loaves. Coffee and teatime became an important repast for all classes of society. From this long-gone era, we have inherited many of the recipes still savored today.

In this book, the specialty cakes span a wide spectrum of flavors. They include streusel-topped and fruit-filled batter cakes, elegant fluted Bundt cakes, healthful fruit-and-nut-embellished loaf cakes, aromatic yeast cakes, and delectable dessert cakes. Savory versions of classic recipes are updated with sun-dried tomatoes, cured olives, fresh rosemary, and lavender. For baking, a variety of pans provide decorative shapes. Antique fluted tube molds with their center cylinder may be filled with flowers or berries for a regal centerpiece on a pedestal plate.

These cakes are perfect for breakfast, brunch, or afternoon, accompanied with coffee, English or herbal teas, hot chocolate, or even cold milk, smoothies, or lemonade. Savory delights include focaccia, fougasse, and polenta cakes to serve as lunchtime or picnic fare. Rich, sweet cakes fill the role of a true dessert. They are usually served unfrosted, but may be enhanced with whipped cream or ice cream.

Baking your own coffee cakes is a rewarding endeavor. May you enjoy the satisfaction of turning out your own fresh-baked sweets and savories.

—Lou Seibert Pappas

baking techniques

**OFFEE CAKES DIVIDE INTO TWO MAIN STYLES:** quick cakes leavened by baking powder and/or baking soda, and those risen by yeast.

**QUICK CAKES:** Here are some basic tips to help achieve a quality product when making coffee cakes with baking powder and baking soda.

Baking powder and baking soda allow batters to rise and achieve a light texture. They are always mixed with flour to disperse them evenly in the finished product. When combined with liquid, baking powder and baking soda give off carbon dioxide, which forms bubbles in the batter. During baking, the flour and egg proteins set around the bubbles, creating a lightened texture. Baking soda, or sodium bicarbonate, is always used with acid ingredients, as the chemical interaction between the two causes leavening. When a recipe calls for buttermilk, yogurt may be used. Or, you may substitute sour milk. To prepare it, put 1 tablespoon freshly squeezed lemon juice or distilled white vinegar into a 1-cup measure and fill it to the 1-cup mark with fresh milk; stir to blend.

It is important to have all the ingredients at room temperature. Measure accurately, using glass cups for liquid measures and metal ones for dry ingredients. Sifting is no longer necessary with flour, though you should stir the flour to aerate it before measuring. To measure, spoon the flour into the measuring cup and then level it off rather than dipping the cup into the flour to fill it. Dry ingredients should be stirred together to distribute the leavening, salt, and spices, if used; a whisk is best for this. Unbleached all-purpose flour is specified in the recipes in this book, as it has been subjected to less chemical alteration than bleached all-purpose flour.

Unsalted, or sweet, butter is preferable for the best flavor; it also contains less moisture than salted butter. Cream the butter and sugar until light and fluffy when specified. In recipes where the dry ingredients are stirred into an egg and oil batter, do not overmix the ingredients. These recipes can be prepared by hand, though an electric mixer speeds the process. Butter baking pans with a small amount of butter and, when specified, flour the pan with about 1 tablespoon of flour, shaking the pan to coat it evenly, then tap out the excess. An alternative method is to butter the bottom and sides of the pan, line the bottom with a piece of parchment paper, and flour the sides of the pan.

Quick cake batter should be baked immediately after mixing. Allow ample time to preheat the oven. Use an oven thermometer and check for doneness at least 5 to 10 minutes before the specified end of the baking time as ovens vary in accuracy. A convection oven, if you have one, will bake cakes evenly thanks to its rapid air circulation but you will need to make adjustments in the timing. In a convection oven, most quick cakes should be baked at a temperature 25° lower than in a conventional oven, and the cooking time may be 10 to 15 minutes shorter.

To test for doneness, insert a cake tester, a toothpick, or a wooden skewer into the center of the cake; it should come out clean, without flecks of dough adhering to it. The color of the crust should be golden brown, and the cake should just start to pull away from the sides of the pan. Let the cake cool in the pan 5 to 10 minutes after baking to firm up and to allow a slight steaming effect to help free it from the pan. Loosen the edges by inserting a knife between the cake and the pan.

Unmold the cake onto a wire rack by holding the rack upside down on the pan and inverting the pan and rack together. If the cake is to be turned top side up, gently hold it in your hands and turn it, or use a second rack and invert it again.

**YEASTED CAKES**:  Yeast-based coffee cakes demand more time in the kitchen, as most need three to four or more hours from start to finish. A critical factor in making these doughs is the temperature of the water for proofing the yeast. It should be warm—105° to 115°F. Mix the dough thoroughly with a heavy-duty mixer fitted with the paddle attachment or by hand, then knead it by hand for 8 to 10 minutes, or until smooth and elastic. Be careful not to incorporate too much flour into the dough; it should be soft and springy.

Let the dough rise at room temperature—65° to 70°F—for the best texture. Do not let it over-rise, or the texture will become coarse and the dough may collapse. When shaping the dough after the first rise, knead it on a lightly floured board for 1 to 2 minutes, just enough to eliminate the air bubbles and make the dough smooth. When done, yeast cakes should be golden brown, and the loaves should sound hollow when thumped.

**STORING AND SERVING COFFEE CAKES**: Both quick-leavened and yeast-based cakes will keep at room temperature, loosely covered, for 2 to 3 days. Almost all coffee cakes freeze well for up to 1 month. Let them cool just to room temperature, then freeze in resealable heavy-duty plastic freezer bags. To defrost, let stand at room temperature fully wrapped but with the wrap slightly loosened to let moisture escape. Reheat in a preheated 350°F oven for 10 to 15 minutes, depending on the size of the cake.

Frozen single slices of coffee cake may go from the freezer to the microwave for a quick defrost and heating. Do not over-microwave, or the baked product will become tough.

Room-temperature coffee cake tends to toughen in the microwave; instead, reheat it in a preheated 325°F oven until warmed through. Some cakes with chocolate flavoring in them are best eaten slightly warm. Reheat them in a preheated 325°F oven for 10 minutes for best results.

sunday
brunch cakes

**A WARM AND AROMATIC COFFEE** cake is an inviting greeting for family and guests at a mid-morning Sunday brunch. Quick and easy batter cakes may be prepared the day of the brunch, while more elaborate yeast-based cakes may be baked ahead and reheated. A variety of streusel, fruit, and caramel toppings add interest and sweetness to these beauties.

# wild huckleberry–streusel sunday coffee cake

Picking wild huckleberries in the Oregon Cascades was an important summer outing when I was young. Turning the bounty into cakes and tarts was a down-home pleasure. To garner my first job at *Sunset* magazine, I featured this recipe in a food story. This versatile, sublime cake is ideal with a range of other fruits: wild or domestic blueberries, marionberries (also called Marion blackberries), boysenberries, loganberries, raspberries, red currants, or sour cherries. The tart fruit and the crunchy, spicy nut topping interplay for a great duo.

Preheat the oven to 350°F. Butter and flour a 9-inch pie pan.

In a large bowl, cream the butter and sugar with a wooden spoon or an electric mixer until light and fluffy. Add the egg, vanilla, and orange zest, and beat well. In a medium bowl, combine the flour, baking powder, baking soda, and salt. Stir to blend. Add to the creamed mixture alternately with the buttermilk in 2 increments, beating just until smooth. Stir in the berries or cherries. Spread evenly over the batter in the prepared pan.

To make the streusel topping: In a small bowl or a food processor, combine the flour, butter, sugar, and cinnamon. Cut in the butter with your fingers or process until crumbly. Stir in the nuts. Sprinkle evenly over the batter and stud with the nut halves.

continued

4 tablespoons (½ stick) unsalted butter at room temperature

6 tablespoons sugar

1 large egg

1 teaspoon vanilla extract

2 teaspoons grated orange zest

1 cup unbleached all-purpose flour

½ teaspoon baking powder

½ teaspoon baking soda

¼ teaspoon salt

⅓ cup buttermilk

1½ cups fresh wild huckleberries, blueberries, blackberries, boysenberries, loganberries, raspberries, red currants, or pitted sour cherries

continued

# wild huckleberry—streusel sunday coffee cake

CONTINUED

## Streusel Topping

¼ cup unbleached all-purpose flour

2 tablespoons cold unsalted butter, cut into bits

¼ cup sugar

1 teaspoon ground cinnamon

⅓ cup (1½ ounces) chopped pecans or walnuts, plus 10 pecan or walnut halves

Bake for 40 to 45 minutes, or until the cake is golden brown and a cake tester inserted in the center comes out clean. Let cool in the pan for 10 minutes, then unmold right side up on a wire rack. Serve warm or at room temperature, cut into wedges.

*Makes one 9-inch cake; serves 8*

# cranberry-pecan-orange coffee cake

**Piquantly tart cranberries** are layered between an exceptional crunchy crust and a sweet streusel topping in this golden cake. Orange juice concentrate accentuates the fresh berry flavor.

Preheat the oven to 350°F. Butter and flour a 9-inch pie pan.

In a large bowl, cream the butter and sugar with a wooden spoon or electric mixer until light and fluffy. Add the egg and vanilla and beat well. In a medium bowl, combine the flour, baking powder, and salt. Stir to blend. Add to the creamed mixture alternately with the orange juice concentrate in 2 increments, beating just until smooth. Stir in the cranberries and nuts. Spread evenly in the prepared pan.

To make the streusel topping: In a small bowl or a food processor, combine the flour, butter, and sugar. Cut in the butter with your fingers or process until crumbly. Sprinkle evenly over the batter and stud with the nut halves.

Bake for 40 to 45 minutes, or until the cake is golden brown and a cake tester inserted in the center comes out clean. Let cool in the pan for 10 minutes, then unmold right side up on a wire rack. Serve warm or at room temperature, cut into wedges.

*Makes one 9-inch cake; serves 8*

4 tablespoons (½ stick) unsalted butter at room temperature

½ cup sugar

1 large egg

1 teaspoon vanilla extract

1 cup unbleached all-purpose flour

1 teaspoon baking powder

¼ teaspoon salt

⅓ cup undiluted frozen orange juice concentrate, thawed

1½ cups fresh or frozen cranberries

⅓ cup (1½ ounces) chopped pecans

## Streusel Topping

¼ cup unbleached all-purpose flour

2 tablespoons cold unsalted butter, cut into bits

¼ cup sugar

½ cup pecan halves

# raspberry-almond coffee cake

## Streusel Topping

3 tablespoons unbleached all-purpose flour

3 tablespoons sugar

1½ tablespoons cold unsalted butter, cut into bits

¼ teaspoon freshly grated or ground nutmeg

½ cup (2 ounces) sliced almonds


10 tablespoons (1 stick plus 2 tablespoons) unsalted butter at room temperature

¾ cup sugar

2 large eggs

1 teaspoon vanilla extract

2 teaspoons grated lemon zest

¾ cup plain yogurt or buttermilk

2 cups unbleached all-purpose flour

1 teaspoon baking powder

½ teaspoon baking soda

¼ teaspoon salt

2 cups fresh raspberries or other berries or pitted sour cherries

**In this delicious old-fashioned** coffee cake, tart, juicy raspberries counterbalance a crunchy topping. Blueberries, blackberries, loganberries, and cranberries are also great choices to stand in for the raspberries.

Preheat the oven to 350°F. Butter and flour a 10-inch springform pan.

To make the streusel topping: In a medium bowl or a food processor, combine the flour, sugar, butter, and nutmeg. Cut in the butter with your fingers or process until crumbly. Stir in the almonds.

In a large bowl, cream the butter and sugar with a wooden spoon or an electric mixer until light and fluffy. Add the eggs, one at a time, beating well. Add the vanilla, lemon zest, and yogurt or buttermilk, beating just until smooth. In a medium bowl, combine the flour, baking powder, baking soda, and salt. Stir to blend. Gradually add the dry ingredients to the butter mixture, beating just until blended. Spread the batter evenly in the prepared pan. Scatter the berries or cherries evenly over the batter and sprinkle evenly with the streusel.

Bake for 55 minutes to 1 hour, or until the cake is golden brown and a cake tester inserted in the center comes out clean. Let cool in the pan on a wire rack for 10 minutes, then remove the pan sides. Serve warm or at room temperature, cut into wedges.

**Makes one 10-inch cake; serves 10 to 12**

# peach-cashew coffee cake

**This light butter cake** encases decorative peach slices under a crunchy cashew topping. A delectable all-around coffee cake, it is perfect for breakfast, mid-afternoon snack, or dessert.

Preheat the oven to 375°F. Butter and flour an 11-inch fluted tart pan with a removable bottom or a 10-inch springform pan.

In a large bowl, cream the butter and granulated sugar until light and fluffy. Add the eggs and amaretto or vanilla and beat until smooth. In another bowl, combine the flour, baking powder, and salt. Stir to blend. Mix the dry ingredients into the butter mixture, beating well until smooth. Turn into the prepared pan. Toss the peaches with the lemon juice and nutmeg and arrange them on top. Sprinkle with the nuts and Demerara or turbinado sugar.

Bake for 25 to 30 minutes, or until golden brown. Let cool in the pan on a wire rack for 10 minutes, then remove the pan sides. Serve warm or at room temperature, cut into wedges or slices, with whipped cream or crème fraîche, if desired.

**Makes one 11-inch cake; serves 10**

½ cup (1 stick) unsalted butter at room temperature

1 cup granulated sugar

3 large eggs

1 tablespoon amaretto liqueur, or 1 teaspoon vanilla extract

1 cup unbleached all-purpose flour

1 teaspoon baking powder

¼ teaspoon salt

4 peaches, peeled, pitted, and cut into ⅜-inch-thick slices

2 tablespoons freshly squeezed lemon juice

¼ teaspoon freshly grated or ground nutmeg

½ cup (2 ounces) roasted cashews or slivered almonds

2 tablespoons Demerara or turbinado sugar

Whipped cream or crème fraîche for serving (optional)

# plum–polka dot caramel cake

4 tablespoons (½ stick) unsalted butter at room temperature

⅓ cup firmly packed light brown sugar

2 large eggs

½ teaspoon vanilla extract

⅔ cup unbleached all-purpose flour

¼ teaspoon freshly grated or ground nutmeg

¼ teaspoon salt

6 plums or apricots, halved and pitted, or 3 nectarines, pitted and sliced, or 3 peaches or pears, peeled, pitted or cored and sliced

## Streusel Topping

2 tablespoons firmly packed light brown sugar

2 teaspoons unbleached all-purpose flour

2 teaspoons cold unsalted butter, cut into bits

⅓ cup (1½ ounces) slivered or sliced almonds

*A spicy cake strewn* with toasty almonds and flavored with brown sugar, puffs up between tangy plum or apricot halves for this easy-to-bake breakfast delight. The scalloped sides of a tart pan lend a decorative touch to the cake wedges.

Preheat the oven to 375°F. Butter and flour a 10-inch fluted tart pan with a removable bottom.

In a large bowl, cream the butter and brown sugar with a wooden spoon or an electric mixer until light and fluffy. Beat in the eggs and vanilla until smooth. In a medium bowl, combine the flour, nutmeg, and salt. Stir to blend. Add to the creamed mixture, beating until smooth. Spread evenly in the prepared pan. Arrange the fruit on top, cavity side up.

To make the streusel topping: In a medium bowl or a food processor, combine the brown sugar, flour, butter, and nuts. Cut the butter in with your fingers or process until crumbly. Sprinkle evenly over the batter.

Bake for 25 minutes, or until the cake is golden brown and the fruit is tender. Let cool in the pan on a wire rack for 10 minutes, then remove the pan sides. Serve warm or at room temperature, cut into wedges.

*Makes one 10-inch cake; serves 6 to 8*

# honey-almond coffee cake

1 package active dry yeast

¼ cup warm water (105° to 115°F)

Pinch of granulated sugar, plus ⅓ cup

½ cup milk

8 tablespoons (1 stick) unsalted butter

½ teaspoon salt

2½ to 2¾ cups unbleached all-purpose or bread flour

3 large eggs

2 tablespoons grated lemon zest

1 teaspoon almond extract

## Almond Topping

⅓ cup firmly packed light brown sugar

2 tablespoons honey

2 tablespoons unsalted butter

2 tablespoons heavy cream

¾ cup (3 ounces) sliced almonds

*A caramelized almond* topping gilds this lemon-scented yeast cake. It makes a decorative show-stopper when baked in a pizza pan. Cut it into generous wedges for a morning treat. It is worth investing in a rasp-style grater, as it releases more zest than other graters.

In a small bowl, sprinkle the yeast over the water, sprinkle with the pinch of sugar, and stir to dissolve. Let stand until foamy, about 10 minutes.

In a small saucepan, heat the milk and butter over low heat until the butter melts. Combine the ⅓ cup sugar and the salt in a large bowl and pour the milk mixture over; let cool to warm, 105° to 115°F. Stir in the yeast mixture. Using a wooden spoon or a heavy-duty electric mixer, add 1 cup of the flour and beat until smooth. Add the eggs and beat until blended. Beat in the lemon zest and almond extract. Gradually add enough of the remaining 1½ to 1¾ cups flour to make a soft dough. Turn the dough out onto a floured board and knead until smooth and elastic, 8 to 10 minutes.

Place the dough in a lightly buttered bowl, turn to coat, and cover with plastic wrap or a damp tea towel. Let rise in a warm place until doubled in size, about 1½ hours.

Punch down the dough. Turn out onto a floured board and knead lightly until smooth, 1 or 2 minutes. Roll into a 12-inch round. Butter a 14-inch pizza pan. Place the dough on the prepared pan. Cover with a tea towel and let rise until doubled in size, about 1 hour.

Preheat the oven to 350°F. Bake the bread for 15 minutes.

Meanwhile, make the almond topping: In a small saucepan, combine the brown sugar, honey, butter, and cream. Place over medium heat and cook, stirring, until thickened, about 3 minutes. Stir in the almonds. Spread the topping carefully over the bread. Bake 10 to 15 minutes longer, or until nicely browned. Let cool for 5 minutes, then unmold right side up on a wire rack and let cool completely. Cut into wedges to serve.

*Makes one 14-inch cake; serves 10 to 12*

# russian apricot-apple pretzel cake

1 package active dry yeast

¼ cup warm water (105° to 115°F)

Pinch of granulated sugar, plus
    6 tablespoons

½ cup milk

4 tablespoons (½ stick) unsalted
    butter

1 teaspoon vanilla extract

½ teaspoon salt

3 large egg yolks

3 cups unbleached all-purpose flour

## Fruit Filling

1 tablespoon unsalted butter

2 tablespoons granulated sugar

4 Granny Smith apples, peeled,
    cored, and thinly sliced

½ cup chopped dried apricots

1 tablespoon unsalted butter, melted

1 teaspoon ground cinnamon

Confectioners' sugar for dusting

**This decorative pretzel-shaped** loaf has lots of tender poached apple slices and sweet-tart dried apricots encased within a tender crust. The twenty-five-year-old Granny Smith apple tree in my garden produces a bountiful crop that goes into this treat.

In a small bowl, sprinkle the yeast over the warm water, add the pinch of sugar, and stir to dissolve; let stand until foamy, about 10 minutes.

In a small saucepan, heat the milk and butter over low heat until the butter melts and the milk reaches 105° to 115°F. Put 4 tablespoons of the granulated sugar in a large bowl and add the milk mixture. Stir in the vanilla, salt, egg yolks, and yeast mixture and beat with a wooden spoon or a heavy-duty electric mixer until smooth. Gradually add enough of the flour to make a soft dough, beating until smooth after each addition. Turn out on a lightly floured board and knead until smooth and elastic, 8 to 10 minutes.

Place in a buttered bowl, turn to coat, and cover the bowl with plastic wrap or a damp tea towel. Let rise in a warm place until doubled in size, about 1½ hours.

Meanwhile, make the fruit filling: In a large frying pan, heat the butter and granulated sugar over medium heat until melted, stirring constantly. Add the apples, increase the heat to high, and cook, stirring occasionally, until just tender, about 5 minutes. Add the apricots and sauté until heated through, about 1 minute. Remove from the heat and let cool.

Turn the dough out on a floured board and knead lightly until smooth, 1 or 2 minutes. Roll out into a rectangle about 9 inches wide and 28 inches long. Spread with the melted butter. Mix the remaining 2 tablespoons granulated sugar and the cinnamon together and sprinkle evenly over the dough. Spread the fruit filling evenly over the dough. Roll up the dough, starting with a long side. Pinch the edges to seal and place, seam side down, on a buttered baking sheet. Form into a circle, then into a stylized pretzel shape by bringing both ends up to the midpoint of the circle and placing one end over the other. Tuck the ends under the center of the roll. Flatten slightly, cover with a towel, and let rise in a warm place until doubled in size, about 1 hour.

Preheat the oven to 350°F. Bake the cake for 45 minutes, or until golden brown. Transfer the cake to a wire rack to cool. Dust the top with confectioners' sugar shaken through a sieve and cut into slices to serve.

*Makes 1 large cake; serves 12*

# apple-walnut mosaic coffee cake

*A brown sugar batter* cloaks chunky apples, dried cranberries, and walnuts to create a decorative fruit cake that is particularly moist. This cake keeps nicely for 4 to 5 days when refrigerated.

........................................................

Preheat the oven to 350°F. Butter and flour a 10-inch tube pan.

Place the nuts on a rimmed baking sheet and bake for 8 to 10 minutes, or until lightly toasted; let cool.

In a small bowl, combine the whole-wheat and all-purpose flours, baking powder, baking soda, salt, cinnamon, and allspice. Stir well to blend. In a large bowl, combine the eggs, brown sugar, oil, and vanilla and beat with a whisk or an electric mixer until smooth. Stir in the flour mixture just until blended. Stir in the apples, cranberries, and toasted nuts. The batter will be stiff. Spread the batter evenly in the prepared pan.

Bake for 1 hour to 1 hour and 5 to 10 minutes, or until the cake is richly browned and a cake tester inserted in the center of the cake comes out clean. Let cool in the pan for 10 minutes, then unmold right side up on a wire rack. If desired, dust the cake with confectioners' sugar shaken through a sieve. Serve slightly warm or at room temperature, cut into slices.

*Makes one 10-inch tube cake; serves 12 to 16*

1¼ cups (5 ounces) walnuts or pecans, coarsely chopped

1 cup whole-wheat flour

1 cup unbleached all-purpose flour

1 teaspoon baking powder

1 teaspoon baking soda

½ teaspoon salt

2 teaspoons ground cinnamon

½ teaspoon ground allspice

2 large eggs

1½ cups firmly packed light brown sugar

⅔ cup canola oil, or ⅓ cup walnut oil and ⅓ cup canola oil

1 teaspoon vanilla extract

5 large Gala, Granny Smith, Winesap, or other tart apples, peeled, cored, and diced (about 6 cups)

1¼ cups dried cranberries

Confectioners' sugar for dusting (optional)

# lemon-glazed almond cake diamonds

## Lemon Syrup

1 cup sugar

2 teaspoons grated lemon zest

1 stick cinnamon

¼ cup fresh lemon juice

⅓ cup water


6 large eggs, separated

¼ teaspoon salt

¼ teaspoon cream of tartar

1 cup sugar, plus 1 teaspoon

2 teaspoons grated lemon zest

⅓ cup zwieback or graham cracker crumbs

1 teaspoon baking powder

¼ teaspoon almond extract

2 cups (8 ounces) finely ground almonds

**This classic Greek almond** cake, known as *amigthalopeta,* is festive in its diamond shape. It is also lovely served plain, without the syrup. One of my favorite recipes from Greek cuisine, this was given to me by my mother-in-law.

To make the lemon syrup: In a small saucepan, combine all the ingredients. Bring to a boil, stirring, and cook until clear. Remove from the heat and let cool to room temperature.

Preheat the oven to 350°F. Lightly butter and flour a 9-by-13-inch baking pan.

In a large bowl, beat the egg whites with an electric mixer until foamy. Add the salt and cream of tartar and beat until soft peaks form. Gradually add ½ cup of the sugar, beating until stiff, glossy peaks form; set aside. In another large bowl, beat the egg yolks with the same beaters until pale in color, then gradually beat in the remaining ½ cup sugar, beating until thick.

In a cup, mash the 1 teaspoon sugar with the lemon zest. In a small bowl, combine the crumbs with the baking powder and the lemon zest mixture and stir to blend. Stir the crumb mixture into the yolks. Stir in the almond extract and half of the almonds. Fold in the beaten egg white mixture. Gently fold in the remaining nuts and turn into the prepared pan.

Bake until the top springs back when touched lightly and a cake tester inserted in the center comes out clean, about 30 minutes. Transfer the pan to a wire rack. Pour the lemon syrup over the hot cake and let the cake cool completely.

To serve, cut the cake into diamond-shaped pieces by first making lengthwise cuts, then cutting on the diagonal crosswise.

*Makes one 9-by-13-inch cake; serves about 12*

# strawberry coffee cake

8 ounces cream cheese at room temperature

8 tablespoons (1 stick) unsalted butter at room temperature

¾ cup granulated sugar

¼ cup milk

2 large eggs

1 teaspoon vanilla extract

2 cups unbleached all-purpose flour

1 teaspoon baking powder

½ teaspoon baking soda

¼ teaspoon salt

3 cups fresh strawberries, sliced

¼ cup firmly packed brown sugar

½ cup chopped almonds or walnuts

**I have had the pleasure** of joining world traveler and culinary expert Eleanor Ostman, a Midwest friend of Finnish heritage, on many international trips she has led for newspaper food editors, garnering recipes from Capetown, South Africa, to Sydney, Australia. When she relaxes at her family's lakeside Minnesota cabin, a holiday outing involves picking "behemoth berries" at the nearby berry farm. The bounty goes into this luscious berry-laden cake to serve guests.

Preheat the oven to 350°F. Butter and flour a 9-by-13-inch baking pan.

In a large bowl, combine the cream cheese, butter, and granulated sugar, and beat with a wooden spoon or an electric mixer until light and fluffy. Stir in the milk, eggs, and vanilla and beat thoroughly. In a medium bowl, combine the flour, baking powder, baking soda, and salt. Stir to blend. Add to the cheese mixture and beat until smooth. Spread half of the batter in the prepared pan. Scatter the berries evenly over the batter. Dot the remaining batter over the berries. Mix the brown sugar and nuts together and sprinkle evenly over the batter.

Bake for 40 minutes, or until the cake is golden brown and a cake tester inserted in the center comes out clean. Let cool in the pan on a wire rack. Serve warm or at room temperature, cut into squares.

*Makes one 9-by-13-inch cake; serves 12*

# white chocolate cheesecake

6 ounces white chocolate wafers (see note, page 114) or chips

1 pound natural or regular cream cheese at room temperature

¾ cup sugar

3 large eggs at room temperature

1½ teaspoons vanilla extract

¾ cup sour cream at room temperature

## Raspberry Coulis

2 cups fresh raspberries

About 2 tablespoons sugar, or to taste

## Garnishes

2 tablespoons unsweetened cocoa powder

½ cup fresh raspberries

**White chocolate adds** its rich flavor to this snowy cheesecake, and a dusting of cocoa proclaims its chocolate status. It makes a spectacular presentation on a pool of raspberry sauce, garnished with whole berries.

Preheat the oven to 325°F. Butter a 9-inch springform pan.

In a double boiler over barely simmering water, melt the chocolate. Stir to blend and let cool to room temperature.

In a food processor, electric mixer, or large bowl, combine the cheese and sugar and blend until smooth. Mix in the eggs, vanilla, and sour cream. Stir in the melted chocolate until smooth (see note). Pour into the prepared pan.

Bake until the cake is just barely set and the center is still slightly wobbly, about 25 minutes. Let cool in the pan on a wire rack, then refrigerate for at least 2 hours or up to 2 days.

To make the raspberry coulis: In a food processor or blender, purée the raspberries and push them through a sieve. Stir in the sugar.

To serve, spoon the raspberry coulis onto dessert plates. Remove the pan sides of the cheesecake and dust the top with the cocoa pushed through a sieve. Cut the cake into wedges. Place each wedge on a pool of the coulis and garnish with the raspberries.

Makes one 9-inch cake; serves 10

NOTE: It is important to have the cheesecake ingredients and the melted chocolate close to the same temperature when they are combined so that they blend together smoothly. If the temperatures are at extremes, the chocolate can seize, or clump together.

# danish chocolate streusel–swirled coffee cake

**This chocolate-filled sweet** bread always graces our table at the Christmas and Easter holiday seasons. It has been a family favorite since the sixties, when my two oldest children shaped it for a food photo story for *Sunset* magazine. Sometimes an almond paste filling replaces the chocolate one.

In a small bowl, sprinkle the yeast over the warm water. Add the pinch of sugar, stir to dissolve, and let stand until foamy, about 10 minutes.

In a large bowl, beat the 6 tablespoons sugar, the butter, salt, and vanilla or cardamom together with a wooden spoon or a heavy-duty electric mixer until light and fluffy. Add the eggs and beat well. Add 1 cup of the flour and beat until smooth. Add the milk, then gradually add 2 cups of the flour, 1 cup at a time, beating well. Stir in the yeast mixture. Gradually add enough of the 1½ to 2 cups remaining flour to make a soft dough. Turn out on a floured board and knead until smooth and elastic, 8 to 10 minutes. Place in a buttered bowl, turn to coat, and cover with plastic wrap or a damp tea towel. Let rise in a warm place until doubled in size, about 1½ hours.

To make the chocolate streusel: In a medium bowl or a food processor, mix the sugar, flour, butter, cocoa, and cinnamon together. Cut the butter in with your fingers or process until crumbly.

*continued*

1 package active dry yeast

¼ cup warm water (105° to 115°F)

Pinch of sugar, plus 6 tablespoons

12 tablespoons (1½ sticks) unsalted butter at room temperature

½ teaspoon salt

2 teaspoons vanilla extract, or ½ teaspoon ground cardamom

3 large eggs

4½ to 5 cups unbleached all-purpose flour

1 cup warm milk (105° to 115°F)

## Chocolate Streusel

⅔ cup sugar

¼ cup unbleached all-purpose flour

3 tablespoons cold unsalted butter, cut into bits

2 tablespoons unsweetened cocoa powder

1 teaspoon ground cinnamon

1 egg white, beaten until foamy

3 tablespoons sliced almonds

# danish chocolate streusel–swirled coffee cake

CONTINUED

Punch down the dough and turn it out on a lightly floured board and knead lightly until smooth, 1 or 2 minutes. Cut the dough in half. Roll one half into a 10-by-14-inch rectangle. Spread evenly with half of the chocolate streusel. Roll up and place, seam side down, on a buttered baking sheet. Repeat with the remaining dough and filling, placing the loaf on a separate buttered baking sheet. With clean scissors, snip each loaf at ¾-inch intervals, cutting three-fourths of the way through the dough. Starting at one end, pull and twist each cut slice on its side to lie flat on alternate sides. Cover with a towel and let rise in a warm place until doubled in size, about 45 minutes.

Preheat the oven to 350°F. Brush the loaves with the egg white and sprinkle with the nuts. Place in the oven, reduce the heat to 325°F, and bake for 30 to 35 minutes, or until golden brown. Transfer the loaves to wire racks to cool completely. Cut into ¾-inch-thick slices to serve. Or, wrap and freeze for up to 2 months.

*Makes 2 loaves*

**ALMOND PASTE FILLING VARIATION:** In a small bowl, combine 8 ounces almond paste, 4 tablespoons (½ stick) unsalted butter at room temperature, 2 tablespoons sugar, ⅓ cup (1½ ounces) finely chopped almonds, and 1 egg. Beat until blended. Use instead of the chocolate streusel.

# sticky caramel pinwheel cake

**Mom's sticky cinnamon** buns were a childhood favorite that vanished almost instantly though she always made a big double batch. Besides being a morning breakfast treat, they were also a favorite for Sunday supper with a fresh fruit salad and hot chocolate. Sometimes a few leftover rolls went into a bread pudding. I love the rolls reheated so the edges get toasty. To turn out a big round coffee cake, bake the sticky buns in a rimmed pizza pan. This is a fail-proof winning sweet roll with any age.

. . . . . . . . . . . . . . . . . . . . . . . . . .

In a small bowl, sprinkle the yeast over the warm water, add the pinch of sugar, and stir to dissolve. Let stand until foamy, about 10 minutes.

In a small saucepan, heat the milk and butter over low heat until the butter melts. Pour into a large bowl and stir in the $\frac{1}{3}$ cup granulated sugar, the salt, and vanilla; let cool to warm (105° to 115°F). Stir in the yeast mixture. Add the eggs, one at a time, and beat until smooth using a wooden spoon or a heavy-duty electric mixer. Gradually beat in enough of the flour to make a soft dough. Turn out onto a floured board and knead until smooth and elastic, 8 to 10 minutes. Place in a buttered bowl, turn to coat, and cover with plastic wrap or a damp tea towel. Let rise in a warm place until doubled in size, about $1\frac{1}{2}$ hours.

Preheat the oven to 350°F. Lightly butter a 9-by-13-inch baking pan or a 14-inch pizza pan with a $\frac{1}{2}$-inch rim.

continued

1 package active dry yeast

¼ cup warm water (105° to 115°F)

Pinch of granulated sugar, plus ⅓ cup

½ cup milk

6 tablespoons unsalted butter

½ teaspoon salt

1 teaspoon vanilla extract

2 large eggs

2½ to 2¾ cups unbleached all-purpose flour

## Caramel Coating

2½ tablespoons unsalted butter

¼ cup light corn syrup

⅔ cup firmly packed light brown sugar

¾ cup (3 ounces) pecans or coarsely chopped walnuts (optional)

1 tablespoon unsalted butter, melted

⅓ cup firmly packed light brown sugar mixed with 1 teaspoon ground cinnamon

# sticky caramel pinwheel cake

CONTINUED

To make the caramel coating: Put the butter, corn syrup, and brown sugar in the baking or pizza pan. Heat in the oven, stirring once or twice, just until the butter melts and the mixture bubbles, 5 to 8 minutes. Spread the coating evenly over the bottom of the pan. Optionally, scatter the nuts over the coating. Let cool to room temperature.

Meanwhile, turn the dough out onto a lightly floured board and knead lightly until smooth, 1 or 2 minutes. Roll into a 10-by-12-inch rectangle. Spread with the melted butter and sprinkle evenly with the brown sugar and cinnamon mixture. Roll up from a long side. Cut into ¾-inch-thick slices. Place the slices, lying flat, ¾ inch apart in the caramel-coated pan. Cover with a tea towel. Let rise in a warm place until doubled in size, about 1 hour.

Preheat the oven to 350°F. Bake the cake for 25 to 30 minutes, or until golden brown. Immediately turn upside down on wire racks and lift the pan off. Let cool slightly. Pull the rolls apart and serve warm.

Makes one 9-by-13-inch or one 14-inch round cake (16 rolls); serves 16

# chocolate angel cake

**As a finale** to a family Sunday brunch, a wedge of this light and flavor-packed angel cake delights any age. It also makes a delectable dessert topped with vanilla bean or coffee ice cream and fresh raspberries.

14 large egg whites

1½ teaspoons cream of tartar

½ teaspoon salt

4 teaspoons water

2 cups sugar

1½ teaspoons vanilla extract

1 cup cake flour

½ cup unsweetened cocoa powder

2 tablespoons instant coffee powder

Preheat the oven to 375°F. In a large bowl, beat the egg whites with an electric mixer until frothy, then beat in the cream of tartar, salt, and water. Beat until soft peaks form, then gradually beat in 1¼ cups of the sugar and the vanilla extract, beating until stiff, glossy peaks form. In a medium bowl, sift the flour, the remaining ¾ cup sugar, the cocoa, and coffee powder together to blend. Gradually fold this mixture into the egg whites. Pour into a 10-inch tube pan with a removable bottom and smooth the top.

Bake for about 35 minutes, or until the top of the cake springs back when lightly touched and a cake tester inserted in the center of the cake comes out clean. Let cool completely upside down on a rack. To serve, remove from the pan and cut into wedges.

*Makes one 10-inch cake; serves 14*

# everyday morning cakes

**FOR BREAKFAST EITHER ON THE** run or in a relaxed mode, a sturdy square of fruit- and nut-studded coffee cake makes a healthful start to the day. These cakes offer well-rounded nutrition, as they incorporate whole grains, cereals, dried fruit, and nuts. For ease in presenting individual servings, use a microwave to reheat a frozen slice.

# morning glory breakfast cake

½ cup quick-cooking or old-fashioned rolled oats

2 large eggs

⅔ cup firmly packed dark brown sugar

1½ cups low-fat plain yogurt or buttermilk

3 tablespoons dark molasses

1 teaspoon vanilla extract

1 cup unbleached all-purpose flour

1 cup whole-wheat flour

2 teaspoons baking soda

¾ teaspoon salt

1 cup wheat bran

2 large carrots, peeled and shredded (2½ cups)

1 large tart apple, peeled, cored, and shredded (1¼ cups)

*A favorite local coffeehouse* gained renown for its Morning Glory muffins, chock-full of shredded carrots, nuts, coconut, and raisins. This variation with shredded apple, blueberries, and dried cherries contains no butter or oil, yet is particularly moist. It is a great breakfast companion with a fruit smoothie. I cut it into slices and freeze the whole batch, then reheat a few pieces daily for breakfast.

Preheat the oven to 350°F. Butter and flour a 9-by-13-inch baking pan.

Spread the rolled oats on a baking sheet and bake for 8 to 10 minutes, or until lightly toasted; remove from the oven and let cool.

In a large bowl, beat the eggs and brown sugar with a whisk or an electric mixer until light and fluffy. Beat in the yogurt or buttermilk, molasses, and vanilla. In a medium bowl, combine the flours, baking soda, salt, wheat bran, and toasted oats. Stir to blend. Add the dry ingredients to the egg mixture and mix just until blended. Stir in the carrots, apple, blueberries, nuts, coconut, and dried fruit. Spread evenly in the prepared pan. Sprinkle the cinnamon sugar evenly over the batter.

Bake for 25 to 30 minutes, or until the cake is golden brown and a cake tester inserted in the center comes out clean. Let cool in the pan on a wire rack. Serve warm, cut into squares or strips.

Makes one 9-by-13-inch cake; serves 12

NOTE: *Toasting and skinning hazelnuts:* Place the nuts in a baking pan and bake in a preheated 325°F oven for 8 to 10 minutes, or until lightly toasted. Let cool for a minute, then place the nuts in a towel and rub them to remove as much skin as possible. Or, hold a handful of nuts over the sink and rub them together with both hands, letting the skins fall away.

MUFFIN VARIATION: Using an ice cream scoop, scoop out mounds of batter and drop into paper-lined large (2 ¾ inches in diameter) muffin cups. Bake in a preheated 375°F oven for 20 minutes, or until a cake tester inserted in the center of a muffin comes out clean. Makes 12 large muffins.

1 cup fresh or frozen blueberries

½ cup hazelnuts, toasted, skinned, and chopped (see note), or chopped walnuts or pecans

½ cup sweetened flaked coconut

½ cup dried cherries, cranberries, or golden raisins

1 tablespoon granulated sugar mixed with 1 teaspoon ground cinnamon

# banana, macadamia nut, and coconut coffee cake

**Toasty sweet macadamia nuts** and cinnamon sugar top this flavorful banana cake laced with flaky coconut. It is especially moist. Select well-ripened (black-speckled) sugar-sweet bananas for best flavor.

Preheat the oven to 350°F. Butter and flour a 9-inch springform pan or round cake pan.

In a large bowl, combine the flour, salt, baking powder, baking soda, and brown sugar. Stir to blend. In a blender or food processor, combine the bananas, eggs, oil, rum or amaretto, sour cream, and vanilla and blend until smooth. Add the banana mixture to the dry ingredients and beat until smooth. Stir in the coconut. Spread evenly in the prepared pan and sprinkle evenly with the nuts. Sprinkle the cinnamon sugar evenly over the batter.

Bake for 30 to 35 minutes, or until the cake is golden brown and a cake tester inserted in the center comes out clean. Let cool in the pan on a wire rack, then remove the pan sides. Serve warm or at room temperature, cut into wedges.

*Makes one 9-inch cake; serves 10*

2 cups unbleached all-purpose flour

½ teaspoon salt

2 teaspoons baking powder

½ teaspoon baking soda

¾ cup firmly packed dark brown sugar

1¼ cups mashed bananas (about 2½ large ripe bananas)

2 large eggs

⅓ cup extra-virgin olive oil (choose a buttery, mild one) or canola oil

2 tablespoons dark rum or amaretto liqueur

½ cup sour cream

1½ teaspoons vanilla extract

½ cup sweetened flaked coconut

½ cup (1½ ounces) chopped macadamia nuts or pecan halves

1 tablespoon granulated sugar mixed with 1 teaspoon ground cinnamon

# caramel-oatmeal-walnut coffee cake

1½ cups boiling water

1 cup quick-cooking or old-fashioned rolled oats

6 tablespoons unsalted butter at room temperature

⅔ cup firmly packed light brown sugar

3 tablespoons dark molasses

2 large eggs

1 teaspoon vanilla extract

1 cup unbleached all-purpose flour

⅔ cup whole-wheat flour

1 teaspoon baking powder

1 teaspoon baking soda

½ teaspoon salt

1 teaspoon ground cinnamon

½ teaspoon ground ginger

¼ teaspoon freshly grated or ground nutmeg

*A broiled caramel frosting* strewn with coconut and pecans gilds this homey, spicy breakfast cake for a treat with a frothy cappuccino or steaming latte.

Preheat the oven to 350°F. Butter and flour a 9-inch square baking pan.

In a medium bowl, pour the boiling water over the rolled oats and let stand until cooled to room temperature. In a large bowl, cream the butter and sugar together with a wooden spoon or an electric mixer until light and fluffy. Beat in the molasses, eggs, vanilla, and oats mixture. In a medium bowl, combine the flours, baking powder, baking soda, salt, cinnamon, ginger, and nutmeg. Stir to blend. Add the dry ingredients to the creamed mixture, beating until smooth. Spread evenly in the prepared pan.

Bake for 30 minutes, or until the cake is golden brown and a cake tester inserted in the center comes out clean.

Just before the cake is done, make the caramel topping: In a small saucepan, combine the butter, brown sugar, and half-and-half or cream. Heat over medium heat, stirring, until the butter and sugar are melted and the mixture is bubbly. Stir in the coconut and nuts.

Remove the cake from the oven and preheat the broiler. Spread the caramel topping evenly over the cake. Place the cake under the broiler 4 inches from the heat source and broil until the topping bubbles and browns, 1 to 2 minutes. Let cool in the pan on a wire rack. Cut into squares to serve.

Makes one 9-inch cake; serves 8

## Caramel Topping

4 tablespoons (½ stick) unsalted butter

½ cup firmly packed brown sugar

3 tablespoons half-and-half or heavy (whipping) cream

½ cup shredded sweetened coconut

¾ cup (3 ounces) chopped pecans or walnuts

# pecan streusel coffee cake

## Streusel Topping

4 tablespoons (½ stick) cold unsalted butter, cut into bits

⅓ cup unbleached all-purpose flour

½ cup firmly packed light brown sugar

1 teaspoon ground cinnamon

1 cup (4 ounces) pecan halves

4 tablespoons (½ stick) unsalted butter at room temperature

½ cup firmly packed light brown sugar

½ cup granulated sugar

2 large eggs

1 teaspoon vanilla extract

2 cups unbleached all-purpose flour

1 teaspoon baking powder

1 teaspoon baking soda

¼ teaspoon salt

1 cup buttermilk or low-fat plain yogurt

**Toasty pecans and brown** sugar streusel compose a crunchy sweet topping for this classic coffee cake.

Preheat the oven to 350°F. Butter a 9-inch springform pan and line the bottom with a round of parchment paper.

To make the streusel topping: In a medium bowl or a food processor, combine the butter, flour, brown sugar, and cinnamon. Cut the butter in with your fingers or process until the mixture forms coarse crumbs. Stir in the nuts and set aside.

In a large bowl, cream the butter and sugars with a wooden spoon or an electric mixer until light and fluffy. Add the eggs and vanilla and beat until smooth. In a medium bowl, combine the flour, baking powder, baking soda, and salt. Stir to blend. Add to the creamed mixture alternately with the buttermilk or yogurt in 2 increments. Beat until smooth. Spread evenly in the prepared pan and sprinkle evenly with the topping.

Bake for 30 to 35 minutes, or until the cake is golden brown and a cake tester inserted in the center comes out clean. Let cool in the pan on a wire rack for 10 minutes, then remove the pan sides and let cool completely. Cut the cake into wedges to serve.

*Makes one 9-inch cake; serves 10*

# blueberry streusel coffee cake

## Streusel Topping

2 tablespoons cold unsalted butter, cut into bits

¼ cup unbleached all-purpose flour

⅓ cup firmly packed light brown sugar

2 teaspoons ground cinnamon

1 cup (4 ounces) walnuts, chopped

½ cup canola oil

½ cup firmly packed light brown sugar

½ cup granulated sugar

2 large eggs

1 teaspoon vanilla extract

1 cup unbleached all-purpose flour

1 cup whole-wheat flour

1 teaspoon baking powder

1 teaspoon baking soda

¼ teaspoon salt

1 cup buttermilk or low-fat plain yogurt

2 cups fresh or frozen blueberries or mixed blackberries, blueberries, and raspberries

*Juicy berries nugget* this easy-to-bake cake that offers a crunchy sweet topping of toasted walnuts and brown sugar streusel.

Preheat the oven to 350°F. Lightly butter and flour a 9-inch spring-form pan.

To make the streusel topping: In a medium bowl or a food processor, combine the butter, flour, brown sugar, and cinnamon. Cut the butter in with your fingers or process until the mixture forms coarse crumbs. Stir in the nuts and set aside.

In a large bowl, combine the oil, sugars, eggs, and vanilla and beat with a wooden spoon or electric mixer until smooth. In a medium bowl, combine the flours, baking powder, baking soda, and salt. Stir to blend. Add to the creamed mixture alternately with the buttermilk or yogurt in 2 increments. Beat until smooth. Stir in the berries. Turn into the prepared pan and sprinkle evenly with the topping.

Bake for 35 to 40 minutes, or until the cake is golden brown and a cake tester inserted in the center comes out clean. Let cool in the pan on a wire rack for 10 minutes, then remove the pan sides and let cool completely. Cut into wedges to serve.

*Makes one 9-inch cake; serves 10*

# persimmon-ginger cake

1½ ripe Hachiya persimmons

1 teaspoon baking soda

1 large egg

½ cup firmly packed light brown sugar

½ cup granulated sugar

1 teaspoon vanilla extract

1 tablespoon brandy or rum

¼ cup milk

1 tablespoon unsalted butter, melted

1 cup plus 2 tablespoons unbleached all-purpose flour

¼ teaspoon salt

1 teaspoon baking powder

1 teaspoon ground cinnamon

½ teaspoon ground allspice

½ teaspoon ground ginger

½ cup chopped walnuts or pecans

⅓ cup finely chopped crystallized ginger

*A surplus of Hachiya persimmons* from my garden inspired this easy-to-mix loaf cake, a perfect mate with afternoon coffee or tea. Slice it thinly and serve plain, or spread it with natural cream cheese and a sprinkle of chopped crystallized ginger. It freezes well for spontaneous entertaining or stores nicely in the refrigerator for 1 week. Because persimmons have a short season, I freeze them whole in resealable plastic freezer bags. To defrost, place them in a bowl of hot water for 1 minute; the skins will peel off with ease.

Preheat the oven to 350°F. Butter and flour 2 small 3½-by-7-inch loaf pans.

Slit the skin of the persimmons with a knife and scoop out the pulp. Mash with a spoon or purée in a blender. You should have 1 cup of pulp. In a small bowl, stir the baking soda into the persimmon pulp and set aside.

In a large bowl, beat the egg and sugars together until blended. Stir in the vanilla, brandy or rum, milk, persimmon pulp, and melted butter. In a medium bowl, combine the flour, salt, baking powder, and spices. Stir to blend. Add the dry ingredients to the persimmon mixture and beat until blended. Mix in the nuts and crystallized ginger. Spread evenly in the prepared pans.

Bake for 45 to 50 minutes, or until the cakes are richly browned and a cake tester inserted in the center of each comes out clean. Let cool in the pans for 10 minutes, then unmold right side up on a wire rack. Let cool completely and serve thinly sliced.

Makes 2 small loaves; serves 12

VARIATION: To make a large cake, double the recipe and bake in a buttered 9-by-13-inch pan for 40 to 45 minutes, or until the cake is richly browned and a cake tester inserted in the center comes out clean.

# cranberry-oatmeal-walnut cake

1½ cups quick-cooking or old-fashioned rolled oats

2 large eggs

½ cup firmly packed light or dark brown sugar

½ cup canola oil

1½ cups buttermilk or low-fat plain yogurt

¼ cup dark molasses

1 teaspoon vanilla extract

1 cup unbleached all-purpose flour

1 cup whole-wheat flour

1 teaspoon baking soda

1 teaspoon baking powder

½ teaspoon salt

2 teaspoons ground cinnamon

2 cups fresh or frozen cranberries

½ cup (2 ounces) chopped walnuts, pecans, or toasted and skinned hazelnuts (see note, page 47)

Scarlet berries dot this healthful cake that is loaded with toasted oatmeal and walnuts.

Preheat the oven to 350°F. Butter and flour a 9-by-13-inch baking pan.

Spread the oats in a rimmed baking sheet and bake for 8 to 10 minutes, or until lightly toasted. Let cool.

In a large bowl, beat the eggs, brown sugar, and oil together until blended and stir in the buttermilk or yogurt, molasses, and vanilla. In a medium bowl, combine the flours, toasted oats, baking soda, baking powder, salt, and 1 teaspoon of the cinnamon. Stir to blend. Add the dry ingredients to the buttermilk mixture and beat for about 1 minute, or until smooth. Stir in the cranberries. Spread evenly in the prepared pan. Toss the nuts and remaining 1 teaspoon cinnamon together and sprinkle evenly over the top.

Bake for 25 to 30 minutes, or until the cake is golden brown and a cake tester inserted in the center comes out clean. Let cool in the pan on a wire rack. Serve warm, cut into squares or strips.

Makes one 9-by-13-inch cake; serves 12

MUFFIN VARIATION: Using an ice cream scoop, scoop out mounds of batter and drop into paper-lined large (2¾ inches in diameter) muffin cups. Bake in a preheated 375°F oven for 20 minutes, or until a cake tester inserted in the center of a muffin comes out clean. Makes 12 large muffins.

# cocoa-dusted cherry granola cake

2 large eggs

½ cup granulated or firmly packed brown sugar

½ cup canola oil

¼ cup honey or molasses

1½ cups buttermilk or low-fat plain yogurt

1 cup unbleached all-purpose flour

1 cup whole-wheat flour or whole-wheat pastry flour

1 teaspoon baking soda

1 teaspoon baking powder

1½ teaspoons ground cinnamon

½ teaspoon salt

1½ cups granola or cereal flakes

1 cup dried cherries

## Cocoa Streusel

¾ cup (3 ounces) chopped walnuts

1 tablespoon unsweetened cocoa powder

2 tablespoons firmly packed brown sugar

2 tablespoons unbleached all-purpose flour

**Cocoa streusel gilds** the top of this crunchy breakfast cake. Sometimes I bake muffins, for individual morning or afternoon treats.

Preheat the oven to 350°F. Butter and flour a 9-by-13-inch baking pan.

In a large bowl, beat the eggs and stir in the granulated sugar, oil, honey or molasses, and buttermilk or yogurt. In a medium bowl, combine the flours, baking soda, baking powder, cinnamon, and salt. Stir to blend. Add the dry ingredients to the buttermilk mixture and beat until blended. Stir in the granola or cereal flakes and dried cherries. Spread evenly in the prepared pan.

To make the cocoa streusel: In a small bowl, toss the nuts, cocoa, brown sugar, and flour together. Sprinkle evenly over the batter. Bake for 30 to 35 minutes, or until the cake is golden brown and a cake tester inserted in the center comes out clean. Let cool in the pan on a wire rack. Serve warm, cut into squares or strips.

**Makes one 9-by-13-inch cake; serves 12**

**MUFFIN VARIATION:** Using an ice cream scoop, scoop out mounds of batter and drop into paper-lined large (2¾ inches in diameter) muffin cups. Bake in a preheated 375°F oven for 20 minutes, or until a cake tester inserted in the center of a muffin comes out clean. Makes 12 large muffins.

# fruit and nut bran cake

*A longtime favorite muffin,* a staple in my house, became the basis for this healthy cranberry, dried plum, and walnut-enriched breakfast bread. The unsweetened wheat bran, found in bulk in natural foods stores, adds lightness and healthy fiber. Cut into squares, the cake freezes beautifully, ready to pop in the microwave or oven to warm. I like to keep several packages of cranberries in the freezer just for this morning treat.

Preheat the oven to 350°F. Butter and flour a 9-by-13-inch baking pan.

In a large bowl, beat the eggs, brown sugar, and oil with a whisk or an electric mixer until smooth. Stir in the buttermilk or yogurt, molasses, and vanilla. In a medium bowl, combine the flours, baking soda, salt, cinnamon, and wheat bran. Stir to blend. Add the dry mixture to the buttermilk mixture and mix just until blended. Stir in the nuts and fruit. Spread evenly in the prepared pan.

Bake for 25 to 30 minutes, or until the cake is golden brown and a cake tester inserted in the center comes out clean. Let cool in the pan on a wire rack. Serve warm, cut into squares or strips.

*Makes one 9-by-13-inch cake; serves 12*

**MUFFIN VARIATION:** Using an ice cream scoop, scoop out mounds of batter and drop into paper-lined large (2¾ inches in diameter) muffin cups. Bake in a preheated 375°F oven for 20 minutes, or until a cake tester inserted in the center of a muffin comes out clean. Makes 12 large muffins.

2 large eggs

½ cup firmly packed light or dark brown sugar

½ cup canola oil

1½ cups buttermilk or low-fat plain yogurt

¼ cup dark molasses

1 teaspoon vanilla extract

1 cup unbleached all-purpose flour

1 cup whole-wheat flour

1½ teaspoons baking soda

½ teaspoon salt

1 teaspoon ground cinnamon

1½ cups wheat bran

½ cup (2 ounces) chopped walnuts, pecans, or toasted and skinned hazelnuts (see note, page 47)

1 cup fresh or frozen cranberries or blueberries, or chopped plums or apricots

1¼ cups prunes (dried plums), pitted and snipped into small pieces

# chocolate nugget–orange flax cake

Orange juice concentrate and orange zest impart a tang to this cereal- and currant-strewn cake. Chocolate chips enhance the topping and add a lovely surprise.

Preheat the oven to 350°F. Butter and flour a 9-by-13-inch baking pan.

In a large bowl, combine the flours, baking soda, baking powder, salt, and granulated sugar. Stir to blend. In a medium bowl, beat the eggs and stir in the oil, buttermilk or yogurt, honey, orange juice concentrate, and orange zest. Add to the dry ingredients and mix just until blended. Mix in the flax cereal and currants or raisins. Turn into the prepared pan and smooth the top. Toss the nuts and chocolate chips together and sprinkle evenly over the top.

Bake for 25 to 30 minutes, or until the cake is golden brown and a cake tester inserted in the center comes out clean. Let cool in the pan on a wire rack. Serve warm, cut into squares or strips.

Makes one 9-by-13-inch cake; serves 12

1 cup unbleached all-purpose flour

1 cup whole-wheat flour or whole-wheat pastry flour

1 teaspoon baking soda

1 teaspoon baking powder

½ teaspoon salt

½ cup granulated or firmly packed brown sugar

2 large eggs

½ cup canola oil

1½ cups buttermilk or low-fat plain yogurt

⅓ cup honey

3 tablespoons thawed frozen orange juice concentrate

2 tablespoons grated orange zest

1½ cups flax cereal

¾ cup dried currants or golden raisins

¾ cup (3 ounces) chopped walnuts or toasted, skinned hazelnuts (see note, page 47)

¾ cup (4 ounces) chocolate chips

# milk chocolate–walnut coffee cake

8 tablespoons (1 stick) unsalted butter at room temperature

½ cup granulated sugar, plus 3 tablespoons

⅓ cup firmly packed light brown sugar

2 large eggs

1 teaspoon vanilla extract

2 cups unbleached all-purpose flour

1½ teaspoons baking powder

½ teaspoon baking soda

¼ teaspoon salt

¾ cup buttermilk or low-fat plain yogurt

2 teaspoons ground cinnamon

6 ounces milk chocolate, finely chopped, or milk chocolate wafers (see note, page 114)

1 cup (4 ounces) chopped walnuts or pecans

**This fine-grained** coffee cake is studded with milk chocolate shavings or wafers and a toasty walnut topping. You may substitute white chocolate or bittersweet wafers.

Preheat the oven to 350°F. Lightly butter and flour a 9-inch springform pan.

In a large bowl, cream the butter and sugars (reserve the 3 tablespoons granulated sugar) together with a wooden spoon or an electric mixer and beat in the eggs and vanilla until smooth. In a medium bowl, combine the flour, baking powder, baking soda, and salt and stir to blend. Stir the dry ingredients into the creamed mixture alternately with the buttermilk or yogurt in 2 increments and beat until the batter is smooth.

Stir together the 3 tablespoons sugar and the cinnamon. Spread half the batter in the prepared pan and sprinkle with half the cinnamon sugar and half the chopped chocolate or wafers. Spread the remaining batter evenly over the top and sprinkle with the remaining cinnamon sugar and chocolate and the nuts.

Bake for 25 to 30 minutes, or until the cake is golden brown and a cake tester inserted in the center comes out clean. Transfer to a wire rack and let cool for 10 minutes. Remove the sides of the pan. Serve the cake warm or at room temperature, cut into wedges.

Makes one 9-inch cake; serves 12

# cinnamon-apple walnut torte

**This fast, favorite** recipe from Schramsberg Winery in Calistoga, California, was featured in my *Winemakers' Cookbook* published in the Eighties. Diced apples, walnuts, and dried cranberries, very lightly bound in an egg and sugar batter, make homey apple pudding-cake. Top with a spoonful of Greek yogurt for a morning treat or embellish with ice cream for an easy guest dinner.

2 eggs

1 cup firmly packed light brown sugar

1 teaspoon vanilla extract

¼ cup unbleached all-purpose flour

⅛ teaspoon salt

2 teaspoons ground cinnamon

1 cup (4 ounces) chopped walnuts or pecans, lightly toasted, if desired

3 Granny Smith apples, peeled, cored, and diced

½ cup dried cranberries or golden raisins

1 tablespoon granulated sugar

Greek yogurt, vanilla ice cream, frozen yogurt, or whipped cream for serving (optional)

Preheat the oven to 350°F. Heavily butter a 9-inch pie pan.

In a large bowl, beat the eggs until frothy with a wooden spoon or an electric mixer and beat in the brown sugar and vanilla until light. In a medium bowl, stir the flour, salt, and 1 teaspoon of the cinnamon together to blend. Stir the flour mixture into the egg mixture.

Reserve ⅓ cup of the nuts for the topping. Mix the remaining nuts, the apples, and cranberries or golden raisins into the batter. Spread evenly in the prepared pan. In a small bowl, mix the granulated sugar, the remaining 1 teaspoon cinnamon, and the reserved nuts together and scatter evenly over the batter.

Bake for 25 to 30 minutes, or until the cake is set and golden brown. Let cool slightly. Serve warm or at room temperature, cut into wedges. Top with yogurt, ice cream, frozen yogurt, or whipped cream, if desired.

Makes one 9-inch torte; serves 8

savory
picnic cakes

WHEN A PICNIC, POTLUCK, OR barbeque is on tap, these free-form savory cakes and breads are satisfying additions to any menu. Flaunting delectable ingredients such as pine nuts, olives, pistachios, lavender, and sun-dried tomatoes, the enticing flavor combinations enhance a wide range of outdoor fare, especially Mediterranean dishes.

# sun-dried tomato–pistachio polenta cake

⅓ cup julienned sun-dried tomatoes

3 tablespoons hot water (optional)

2 large eggs

⅓ cup extra-virgin olive oil

2 tablespoons honey

1 teaspoon dried basil

1 teaspoon dried oregano

1¾ cups unbleached all-purpose flour

¾ cup finely ground polenta or cornmeal

¾ teaspoon salt

1 teaspoon baking powder

½ teaspoon baking soda

¾ cup buttermilk or low-fat plain yogurt

⅔ cup (2½ ounces) unsalted pistachios

½ cup (2 ounces) grated Parmesan cheese

**This savory tomato** herb bread has a delicious polenta and nut crunch in each golden slice. Nicely moist, with a fine, crumbly texture, it is excellent warm or cold. Serve it for an Italian-style brunch, lunch, or buffet party. It is also an ideal complement to a Caesar salad or a lentil or bean soup for a light meal.

Preheat the oven to 375°F. Butter and flour a 9-inch springform pan or pie pan.

If the tomatoes are dry-packed, cover them with the hot water and let steep for 5 to 10 minutes to soften.

In a large bowl, beat the eggs with a whisk or an electric mixer until light. Blend in the oil, honey, and herbs. In a medium bowl, combine the flour, polenta or cornmeal, salt, baking powder, and baking soda. Stir to blend. Stir the dry ingredients into the egg mixture alternately with the buttermilk or yogurt in 2 increments. Beat until smooth. Stir in the tomatoes and any liquid. Reserve 2 tablespoons of the nuts and 2 tablespoons of the cheese for the topping and stir the remainder into the batter. Spread the batter evenly in the prepared pan and sprinkle evenly with the reserved nuts and cheese.

Bake for 30 minutes, or until the cake is golden brown and a cake tester inserted in the center comes out clean. Let cool in the pan for 10 minutes, then unmold right side up on a wire rack. Serve warm or at room temperature, cut into wedges.

*Makes one 9-inch cake; serves 10*

# black olive–pine nut polenta cake

¾ cup golden raisins

2 tablespoons dry Marsala or brandy

2 large eggs

⅓ cup extra-virgin olive oil

2 tablespoons honey

1 tablespoon minced fresh rosemary

1 tablespoon grated lemon zest

1¾ cups unbleached all-purpose flour

¾ cup finely ground polenta or cornmeal

¾ teaspoon salt

1 teaspoon baking powder

½ teaspoon baking soda

¾ cup buttermilk or low-fat plain yogurt

⅔ cup (4 ounces) pine nuts

¾ cup oil-cured black olives, pitted and halved or coarsely chopped

**The salty bite of olives** and sweetness of golden raisins and pine nuts interplay superbly in this savory, tender coffee cake. Serve wedges with a well-brewed cup of Italian roast coffee as a welcome change from sweet cakes, or serve as a hearty, delightful appetizer with wine or beer.

Preheat the oven to 375°F. Butter and flour a 9-inch springform pan or pie pan.

In a small bowl, toss the raisins with the Marsala or brandy and let stand for 10 to 15 minutes.

In a large bowl, beat the eggs with a whisk or an electric mixer until light and blend in the oil, honey, rosemary, and lemon zest. In a medium bowl, combine the flour, polenta or cornmeal, salt, baking powder, and baking soda. Stir to blend. Stir the dry ingredients into the egg mixture alternately with the buttermilk or yogurt in 2 increments, mixing just until smooth. Reserve 3 tablespoons of the nuts and ¼ cup of the olives for the topping and stir the remainder into the batter. Spread the batter evenly in the prepared pan. Sprinkle evenly with the reserved nuts and olives.

Bake for 30 minutes, or until the cake is golden brown and a cake tester inserted in the center comes out clean. Let cool in the pan for 10 minutes, then unmold right side up on a wire rack. Serve warm or at room temperature, cut into wedges.

Makes one 9-inch cake; serves 10

# *ruby grape* focaccia

*A crusty focaccia,* aromatic with lavender and bursting with the sweetness of grapes, is a seductive companion to a cup of dark-roast coffee.

In a large bowl, sprinkle the yeast and the pinch of sugar into the warm water. Stir to dissolve and let stand until foamy, about 10 minutes.

Stir in the room-temperature water and the 1½ tablespoons oil. Add 1 cup of the flour, the 3 tablespoons sugar, the lavender or lemon balm, and salt and mix until smooth using a wooden spoon or a heavy-duty mixer. Beat in the remaining 2 cups flour, ½ cup at a time, until the dough comes together in a loose ball. On a floured board, knead the dough until smooth and elastic, 8 to 10 minutes.

Place the dough in a lightly oiled bowl, turn to coat, and cover with plastic wrap or a damp tea towel. Let rise in a warm place until doubled, about 1½ hours. Punch down, turn out on a lightly floured board, and knead a few times to eliminate air bubbles.

Roll the dough out to fit a rimmed baking sheet. Oil the pan and fit in the dough. With your fingers, dimple the dough by making depressions about 1 inch apart. Brush with olive oil. Push the grapes evenly into the dough (not in the depressions). Cover with a tea towel and let rise until doubled, about 45 minutes.

Preheat the oven to 425°F. Bake the focaccia for 15 to 20 minutes, or until golden brown. Remove from the pan and transfer to wire racks to cool. Serve warm or at room temperature, cut into squares or wedges.

*Makes 1 large rectangular flat bread; serves 12*

1 package active dry yeast

Pinch of sugar, plus 3 tablespoons

¼ cup warm water (105° to 115°F)

1¼ cups water at room temperature

1½ tablespoons olive oil, plus more for brushing

3 cups unbleached all-purpose or bread flour

3 tablespoons fresh lavender blossoms or minced fresh lemon balm, or 2 tablespoons dried lavender blossoms

1½ teaspoons salt

2 cups red seedless grapes

# italian cheese and herb pinwheels

**This fine-textured** brioche-style loaf is laced with a green-and-white pinwheel of herbs and cheeses for a delicious flavor and eye-catching appeal. It makes a hearty loaf for a Tuscan picnic. Or serve warm slices for a salad lunch or soup supper. It is a treasure for a variety of occasions.

Lightly oil 2 rimmed baking sheets.

In a large bowl, sprinkle the yeast and the pinch of sugar over the warm water. Stir to dissolve and let stand until foamy, about 10 minutes.

Add the 2 tablespoons sugar, the salt, and 1 cup of the flour; beat well with a wooden spoon or a heavy-duty electric mixer. Add 3 of the eggs, one at a time, and beat until smooth. Beat in the olive oil or butter and gradually add enough of the remaining 2½ cups flour to make a soft dough. Turn out on a floured board. Knead until smooth and elastic, 8 to 10 minutes. Place in an oiled bowl and turn to coat. Cover with plastic wrap or a damp tea towel. Let rise in a warm place until doubled in size, about 1½ hours.

*continued*

1 package active dry yeast

Pinch of sugar, plus 2 tablespoons

1 cup warm water (105° to 115°F)

1 teaspoon salt

3½ cups unbleached all-purpose flour

4 large eggs

½ cup extra-virgin olive oil, or 8 tablespoons (1 stick) unsalted butter at room temperature

¾ cup (3 ounces) grated romano or Parmesan cheese

½ cup (2 ounces) shredded Asiago cheese

½ cup (2 ounces) shredded Monterey Jack cheese

½ cup mixed minced fresh Italian parsley, basil, chives, and oregano

# italian cheese and herb pinwheels

CONTINUED

Turn out onto a floured board. Knead lightly until smooth, 1 or 2 minutes, and divide in half. Roll out each piece into a rectangle about 10 by 16 inches.

In a small bowl, beat the remaining egg and blend in the cheeses and herbs. Spread half of the cheese filling evenly over each dough rectangle. Roll each up firmly, starting from a long side. Place one loaf on each of the prepared pans, seam side down. With clean scissors, snip each loaf at $1\frac{1}{4}$-inch intervals, cutting three-fourths of the way through the dough. Pull and twist each cut piece to lie flat on an alternate side. Cover with a tea towel and let rise in a warm place until doubled in size, about $1\frac{1}{2}$ hours.

Preheat the oven to 350°F. Bake the loaves for 30 to 35 minutes, or until they are golden brown and sound hollow when thumped. Let cool on the pans for 10 minutes, then transfer from the pans to wire racks. Serve warm or at room temperature, cut into slices.

Makes 2 loaves; serves 20

# gruyère brioche braid

**Nuggets of creamy** cheese stud this buttery egg bread for a superb savory treat. Serve with thinly sliced ham for brunch or lunch, or savor with a glass of red wine.

In a small bowl, sprinkle the yeast over the warm water. Add the pinch of sugar, stir to dissolve, and let stand until foamy, about 10 minutes.

In a large bowl, beat the butter with a wooden spoon or an electric mixer until creamy. Add the 1 tablespoon sugar, the salt, and the 3 eggs, beating well. Add the milk and the yeast mixture. Gradually add the flour, $\frac{1}{2}$ cup at a time, adding just enough to make a soft dough and beating well after each addition. Beat the dough until smooth, satiny, and elastic. Cover the bowl with plastic wrap or a damp tea towel and let rise in a warm place until doubled in volume, about $1\frac{1}{2}$ hours. Punch down, cover, and refrigerate for at least 2 hours or overnight.

To shape, turn the cold dough out on a lightly floured board and knead a few times to soften slightly. Knead in the cheese. Divide into 3 equal portions and roll each portion into a rope about 16 inches long. Place the 3 ropes parallel on a buttered baking sheet, then form them into a braid, pinching the ends together to seal. Cover with a tea towel and let rise in a warm place until doubled in volume, about $1\frac{1}{2}$ hours.

Preheat the oven to 375°F. Brush the dough with the egg-milk mixture. Bake for 30 to 35 minutes, or until the bread is golden brown and sounds hollow when thumped. Let cool on the pan for 10 minutes, then transfer from the pan to a wire rack. Serve warm or at room temperature, cut into slices.

**Makes 1 large loaf; serves 8 to 10**

1 package active dry yeast

¼ cup warm water (105° to 115°F)

Pinch of sugar, plus 1 tablespoon

10 tablespoons (1 stick plus 2 tablespoons) unsalted butter at room temperature

1 teaspoon salt

3 large eggs

½ cup warm milk (105° to 115°F)

3¼ cups unbleached all-purpose flour

1½ cups (6 ounces ) shredded Gruyère cheese

1 large egg yolk beaten with 1 tablespoon milk

# olive-herb-potato fougasse

1 pound russet potatoes (whole, scrubbed)

1 package active dry yeast

½ cup warm water (105° to 115°F)

1 teaspoon packed light brown sugar or honey

2 tablespoons extra-virgin olive oil, plus 1 tablespoon for brushing

2 tablespoons minced fresh sage or rosemary

3½ cups unbleached all-purpose flour

2 teaspoons salt

⅓ cup oil-packed olives, pitted and halved

**In the south of** France, bakers give *pain ordinaire* dough a free-form shape by slashing and stretching it to resemble a tree-of-life design or a ladder. Studded with olives and herbs, it makes a fun pull-apart loaf known as fougasse. Mashed potatoes in the dough contribute an especially light crumb.

In a medium saucepan, cover the potatoes with cold water and bring to a boil. Reduce the heat to a simmer, cover, and cook for 30 minutes, or until tender.

Meanwhile, preheat the oven to 300°F. Drain the potatoes, reserving 1 cup of the liquid; let the water cool to room temperature. Place the potatoes on a baking sheet and let dry in the oven for 10 minutes.

Meanwhile, in a small bowl, sprinkle the yeast over the warm water. Stir in the brown sugar or honey until dissolved and let stand until foamy, about 10 minutes.

Peel the potatoes and place them in a large bowl; beat with an electric mixer or use a potato masher to mash them. Stir in the reserved potato water and 2 tablespoons of the olive oil. Add the yeast mixture, herbs, 1 cup of the flour, and the salt and mix until smooth. Stir in the remaining 2½ cups flour ½ cup at a time until the dough comes together in a loose ball. On a floured board, knead the dough until smooth and elastic, 8 to 10 minutes. The dough will be quite soft.

*continued*

# olive-herb-potato fougasse

CONTINUED

Put the dough in an oiled bowl, turn to coat, and cover with plastic wrap or a damp tea towel. Let rise in a warm place until doubled, about 1½ hours. Punch the dough down, turn it out onto a lightly floured board, and knead a few times to eliminate air bubbles. Roll the dough into a rectangle about 10 by 14 inches and place on an oiled baking sheet. Use a dough scraper or clean razor blade to make 4 or 5 diagonal cuts, each about 4 inches long, slanting downward on one side of an imaginary center line. Make matching cuts on the other side of the line. Open the cuts by pulling gently. Do not cut through or tear the encircling piece of dough. Brush with the remaining 1 tablespoon olive oil and stud the surface with the olives. Cover with a tea towel and let rise until doubled.

Preheat the oven to 425°F. Bake for 20 to 25 minutes, or until golden brown. Transfer the loaf to a wire rack and let cool. Serve warm or at room temperature, and pull apart to serve.

Makes 1 large loaf; serves 16

# french galette with cherry-almond topping

**Shaped like a pizza,** this buttery bread is punctuated with tart cherries and toasted almonds. Serve it warm with Gouda goat cheese and steaming Mocha-Java coffee or big bowls of hot chocolate for a delicious breakfast treat. Or offer for dessert with a cup of French roast or espresso.

In a large bowl, sprinkle the yeast over the warm water. Add the pinch of sugar and stir until dissolved. Let stand until foamy, 10 minutes.

Using a wooden spoon, or a heavy-duty electric mixer, beat in the butter, the 3 tablespoons sugar, the egg, vanilla, nutmeg, and salt. Gradually add enough of the flour, ½ cup at a time, to make a soft dough. Beat well. Turn out onto a floured board and knead until smooth and elastic, 8 to 10 minutes. Place in a buttered bowl, turn to coat, and cover with plastic wrap or a damp tea towel. Let rise in a warm place until doubled in size, about 1 hour.

Lightly butter a 14-inch pizza pan. Punch down the dough and turn out on a floured board. Knead lightly until smooth, 1 or 2 minutes. Roll out into a 15-inch round and place in the prepared pan. Form a rim around the edge of the dough. For the topping, spread the dough with the 2 tablespoons butter and sprinkle with the 3 tablespoons sugar. Scatter the cherries and nuts evenly over the dough. Cover with a tea towel and let stand in a warm place for 20 minutes to rise slightly.

Meanwhile, preheat the oven to 500°F. Bake for 6 to 7 minutes or until the crust is golden brown. Transfer from the pan to a wire rack and let cool. Serve warm, cut into wedges.

*Makes one 14-inch flat bread; serves 4*

1 package active dry yeast

6 tablespoons warm water (105° to 115°F)

Pinch of sugar, plus 3 tablespoons

4 tablespoons (½ stick) unsalted butter at room temperature

1 large egg

1 teaspoon vanilla extract

¼ teaspoon freshly grated or ground nutmeg

½ teaspoon salt

1⅔ cups unbleached all-purpose flour

## Topping

2 tablespoons unsalted butter at room temperature

3 tablespoons sugar

⅓ cup dried cherries

½ cup (2 ounces) slivered or sliced almonds

# *sunflower seed* pull-apart focaccia

**This loaf is dramatic** to serve, as the sunflower shape pulls apart with ease into tender, springy pieces for individual servings. Coating your fingers with olive oil instead of flour makes the dough easy to handle when shaping. If chestnut flour is available, it is a wonderful nut-scented variation.

1 package active dry yeast

¼ cup warm water (105° to 115°F)

Pinch of sugar or drop of honey

1¼ cups water at room temperature

1 tablespoon honey

2 tablespoons extra-virgin olive oil, plus more for brushing

3¼ cups unbleached all-purpose flour

1½ teaspoons salt

1 tablespoon aniseed or minced fresh rosemary

¼ cup sunflower seeds

2 dozen oil-cured black olives, pitted, or ½ cup seedless red grapes

In a large bowl, sprinkle the yeast over the warm water. Add the sugar or honey, stir to dissolve, and let stand until foamy, about 10 minutes.

Stir in the room-temperature water, the 1 tablespoon honey, and the 2 tablespoons olive oil. Using a wooden spoon or a heavy-duty mixer, add 1 cup of the flour and the salt and mix until smooth. Grind the aniseed in a mortar to release the flavors, if using. Beat the aniseed or rosemary into the mixture. Beat in the remaining 2¼ cups flour, ½ cup at a time, until the dough comes together in a loose ball.

Using a heavy-duty mixer fitted with the dough hook, or by hand on a lightly floured board, knead the dough until smooth and elastic, 8 to 10 minutes. Put the dough in a lightly oiled bowl, turn to coat, and cover with plastic wrap or a damp tea towel. Let rise in a warm place until doubled, about 1½ hours.

*continued*

# sunflower seed pull-apart focaccia

### CONTINUED

Lightly oil a 14-inch pizza pan. Punch down the dough, turn out on a lightly floured board, and knead until smooth, 1 or 2 minutes. Roll the dough out into a 14-inch round and place on the pizza pan. With a glass turned upside down, cut out a 3-inch round in the center of the dough, then with a pastry scraper or knife, divide the outer circle of dough into fourths. Cut each piece into fourths again to make 16 slices. Twist each cut strip over and lay it flat. Brush the dough with olive oil and sprinkle with the sunflower seeds. Stud the end of each strip with an olive or a grape and place several in the center. Cover with a tea towel and let rise until doubled, about 45 minutes.

Preheat the oven to 425°F. Bake the bread for 20 to 25 minutes, or until golden brown. Transfer the bread from the pan to a wire rack to cool. Serve warm or at room temperature. Pull apart to serve.

*Makes 1 large loaf; serves 12*

**CHESTNUT FLOUR VARIATION**: Substitute ½ cup chestnut flour for ½ cup of the unbleached flour.

# greek almond-crusted citrus loaves

**In Greece, this** toasted almond and sugar-capped yeast bread rings in the New Year. Imbued with citrus zest, it has a lovely feathery texture and hint of sweetness.

In a small bowl, sprinkle the yeast over the warm water, add the pinch of sugar, and stir until dissolved. Let stand until foamy, 10 minutes.

In a large bowl, combine the milk, butter, the 1/3 cup granulated sugar, and salt. Add the eggs, vanilla and almond extracts, orange and lemon zests, and 1 cup of the flour. Using a wooden spoon or a heavy-duty electric mixer, beat until smooth. Add the yeast mixture and 1 more cup of the flour and beat until smooth. Gradually beat in enough of the remaining 2 to 2 1/2 cups flour, 1/2 cup at a time, to make a soft dough. Turn out onto a lightly floured board and knead until smooth and elastic, 8 to 10 minutes. The dough should be soft. Place in a buttered bowl, turn to coat, and cover with plastic wrap or a damp towel. Let rise at room temperature until doubled in size, about 2 hours.

Lightly butter two 9-inch pie pans or 2 baking sheets. Turn the dough onto a floured board and knead lightly until smooth, 1 or 2 minutes. Divide the dough in half and shape into 2 round, flat loaves about 7 inches in diameter and place in the prepared pans. Cover with a tea towel and let rise until doubled in size, about 45 minutes.

Preheat the oven to 350°F. For the topping, brush the loaves with the egg white and sprinkle with the almonds and sugar. Bake for 25 to 30 minutes, or until the loaves are golden brown. Let cool, then transfer from the pans to wire racks. Serve warm, cut into wedges.

*Makes two 9-inch loaves; serves 16*

1 package active dry yeast

1/4 cup warm water (105° to 115°F)

Pinch of granulated sugar, plus 1/3 cup

1 cup warm milk (105° to 115°F)

8 tablespoons (1 stick) unsalted butter, melted

1 teaspoon salt

2 large eggs

2 teaspoons vanilla extract

1/2 teaspoon almond extract

2 tablespoons grated orange zest

1 tablespoon grated lemon zest

4 to 4 1/2 cups unbleached all-purpose flour

## Topping

1 large egg white, lightly beaten

About 3 tablespoons slivered or sliced almonds

2 tablespoons Demerara or turbinado sugar

# filo-wrapped havarti cheesecake

4 sheets frozen filo dough (each about 13 by 17 inches), thawed

3 tablespoons unsalted butter, melted

3 tablespoons dried egg bread or white bread crumbs

One 7-ounce round Havarti cheese

1 tablespoon minced fresh rosemary

3 tablespoons chopped pistachios or pine nuts

3 Comice, red Bartlett, or Anjou pears, or Fuji or Winesap apples

**Crisp layers of filo** dough make a handsome pouf to encase Havarti cheese strewn with pistachios and fresh rosemary. When cut, the creamy cheese oozes to an unctuous spread that is excellent with sliced pears or apples. It is also superb with Fuyu persimmons. Serve on a patio buffet table or carry to a potluck occasion.

Preheat the oven to 350°F. Line a baking sheet with parchment paper.

Stack the filo sheets on a cutting board and trim one end to create a 13-inch square. (Use the cut-off strip for another purpose.) Lay 1 sheet on a clean work surface and cover the remaining dough with a cloth to keep it moist. Brush the filo sheet with some of the butter and sprinkle with 1 tablespoon of the crumbs. Place a second sheet on top of the first and repeat the process. Repeat with the third sheet. Top with the fourth sheet, butter it, and place the cheese in the center. Sprinkle with the rosemary and nuts. Bring the four corners of the square together and twist securely to enclose the cheese. Spread out the ends to form a pouf. Brush the filo with the remaining butter. Place on the prepared baking sheet. Bake now, or cover with plastic wrap and refrigerate for 2 to 3 hours.

Bake for 18 to 20 minutes, or until the filo is golden brown. Remove from the oven and let cool for a few minutes. Serve immediately. Or, let cool completely and let stand at room temperature for up to 4 hours before serving or refrigerate for up to 1 day; reheat in a preheated 350°F oven to serve.

Transfer to a serving platter. Halve, core, and slice the pears or apples and encircle the pastry. Cut into wedges to serve.

### Makes 6 to 8 servings

NOTE: If a round of Havarti is unavailable, select a 4-inch square of Havarti or Samsoe cheese, cut about 1 inch thick.

# italian lavender honey wreaths

Toasting enhances the intriguing lavender scent that pevades this olive oil and honey-flavored bread. The ring shape is both decorative and especially nice for even slicing. If possible, use fresh lavender, though dried lavender works fine out of season.

In a small bowl, sprinkle the yeast over the warm water. Add the pinch of sugar and stir until dissolved. Let stand until foamy, about 10 minutes.

In a small saucepan, heat the milk and lavender over low heat until small bubbles form around the edge of the pan. Remove from the heat and let cool to lukewarm; strain, discarding the lavender.

In a large bowl, combine the flavored milk, olive oil, honey, and salt. Add the 2 eggs and egg yolk, brandy or Cognac, lemon zest, and 1 cup of the flour. Using a wooden spoon or a heavy-duty mixer, beat until smooth. Add the yeast mixture and an additional 1 cup of the flour and beat until smooth. Gradually add the remaining 2½ to 2¾ cups flour, ½ cup at a time, beating well and adding enough to make a soft dough.

Turn out onto a lightly floured board and knead until smooth and elastic, 8 to 10 minutes. The dough should be soft. Put it in a buttered bowl, turn to coat, and cover with plastic wrap or a damp tea towel. Let rise in a warm place until doubled in size, about 2 hours.

*continued*

1 package active dry yeast

¼ cup warm water (105° to 115°F)

Pinch of sugar

1 cup milk

3 tablespoons fresh lavender blossoms, or 2 tablespoons dried lavender blossoms

⅓ cup extra-virgin olive oil

⅓ cup honey

1 teaspoon salt

2 large eggs, plus 1 large egg, separated

1 tablespoon brandy or Cognac

2 tablespoons grated lemon zest

4½ to 4¾ cups unbleached all-purpose flour

⅓ cup (1½ ounces) pine nuts

# *italian lavender* honey wreaths

CONTINUED

Lightly butter 2 rimmed baking sheets. Turn the dough out onto a floured board and knead lightly until smooth, 1 or 2 minutes. Divide the dough in half and shape each piece into a round ball. With your fingers, poke a hole in the center of one. Slip your hands into the hole and stretch the dough to make a ring about 10 inches in diameter. Place on the prepared pan and repeat with the second ball of dough. Cover with a tea towel and let rise in a warm place until doubled in size, about 1 hour.

Preheat the oven to 350°F. In a small bowl, beat the egg white until foamy and brush the rings with it. Sprinkle with the nuts. Bake for 22 to 25 minutes, or until the loaves are golden brown and sound hollow when tapped. Let cool on the pans for 10 minutes, then transfer from the pans to wire racks. Serve warm or at room temperature, cut into slices, or toasted.

*Makes 2 ring-shaped loaves; serves 16 to 20*

**ANISE VARIATION:** Omit the lavender and substitute 2 teaspoons aniseed. Heat the aniseed in the milk until the milk is steaming hot; do not strain.

# garlic-rosemary rounds

*Roasted garlic and fresh* rosemary adorn the crust of this wholesome bread with a robust appeal. It's a winning picnic bread to pair with sliced smoked turkey and Asiago cheese.

In a small bowl, sprinkle the yeast into ½ cup of the warm water. Add the pinch of sugar, stir to dissolve, and let stand until foamy, about 10 minutes.

In a large bowl, combine the whole-wheat flour, ½ cup of the all-purpose flour, and the salt. Add the remaining 2 cups warm water, the honey, and 3 tablespoons of the olive oil. Using a wooden spoon or a heavy-duty electric mixer, beat until smooth. Mix in the yeast mixture and 1 tablespoon of the rosemary. Stir in most or all of the remaining flour, enough to make a soft dough.

Turn the dough out on a lightly floured board and knead until smooth and elastic, 8 to 10 minutes. Place in a buttered bowl, turn to coat, and cover with plastic wrap or a damp tea towel. Let rise in a warm place until doubled in size, about 1½ hours.

Preheat the oven to 325°F. Lightly butter two 9-inch pie pans.

Meanwhile, place the garlic in a small baking dish and rub with 1½ teaspoons of the remaining olive oil. Bake for 30 minutes or until soft; peel and slice. Add the remaining rosemary and 1½ teaspoons olive oil, mixing lightly.

*continued*

2 packages active dry yeast

2½ cups warm water (105° to 115°F)

Pinch of sugar

2 cups whole-wheat flour

3 to 3½ cups unbleached all-purpose flour

2½ teaspoons salt

3 tablespoons honey

4 tablespoons olive oil, plus more for brushing

2 tablespoons minced fresh rosemary

6 unpeeled cloves garlic

# garlic-rosemary rounds

Punch the dough down and turn it out on a lightly floured board. Divide the dough in half and shape into 2 round loaves, kneading out the air bubbles. Place each dough round in the prepared pans. With your finger, poke 6 to 8 indentations around the outer edge of the top surface. Fill the indentations with the garlic mixture, dividing it evenly. Cover with a tea towel and let rise until doubled, about 1 hour. Brush with olive oil.

Increase the oven temperature to 375°F. Bake the loaves for 40 minutes, or until they are golden brown and sound hollow when thumped. Let cool in the pans for 10 minutes, then unmold right side up onto wire racks and let cool completely. Serve cut into wedges.

Makes two 9-inch loaves; serves 12

# pistachio-olive galette

**Pistachios, olives, and golden** raisins adorn this French-style pie to serve warm or at room temperature, cut into fat wedges. If you have a pizza stone, bake the galette on the preheated stone for an extra-crisp crust.

In a large bowl, sprinkle the yeast into the warm water and stir to dissolve. Let stand until foamy, about 10 minutes. Beat in the ¼ cup olive oil, the honey, egg, rosemary, salt, and lemon zest with a wooden spoon or an electric mixer. Gradually add the flour to make a soft dough. Turn out onto a floured board and knead until smooth and elastic, 8 to 10 minutes. Place in an oiled bowl and turn to coat. Cover with plastic wrap or a damp tea towel. Let rise in a warm place until doubled in size, about 1½ hours.

Punch down the dough and turn out on a floured board. Knead lightly until smooth, 1 or 2 minutes. Roll out into a 15-inch round and place in an oiled 14-inch pizza pan or on a baking sheet. Form a rim around the edge. Brush with the 1 tablespoon olive oil and scatter evenly with the olives, nuts, and raisins or apricots. Let stand in a warm place for 30 minutes to rise slightly.

Meanwhile, preheat the oven to 475°F. Bake for 6 to 8 minutes, or until the crust is golden brown. Serve warm, cut into wedges.

*Makes one 14-inch round bread; serves 12*

1 package active dry yeast

6 tablespoons warm water (105° to 115°F)

¼ cup olive oil, plus 1 tablespoon

2 tablespoons honey

1 egg

1 tablespoon minced fresh rosemary

1 teaspoon salt

2 teaspoons grated lemon zest

1⅔ cups unbleached all-purpose flour

½ cup pitted salt-cured black olives

⅓ cup pistachios

⅓ cup golden raisins or diced dried apricots

# bundt
# party cakes

**A FLUTED BUNDT CAKE, RIDING HIGH** on a pedestal plate, makes a striking centerpiece for a special occasion, such as a bridal or baby shower, a birthday lunch, or a holiday fête. Both antique copper molds and contemporary ones come in many designs. Or, you can use a tube pan. Some of these festive cakes are further elaborated with swirled or marbleized batters and/or nut crusts.

# cheese-swirled chocolate bundt cake

**This bountiful, glamorous** party cake is designed as a gala dessert, ideal to pair with espresso or Viennese roast coffee. A ribbon of chocolate chip–dotted cream cheese filling swirls within the rich chocolate cake. The cocoa-sugar topping lends a pretty finishing touch to the dark surface.

Preheat the oven to 325°F. Butter and flour a 10-inch Bundt or tube pan.

To make the cheese filling: In a medium bowl, cream the cheese, granulated sugar, and vanilla until fluffy and beat in the egg. Stir in the chocolate chips and set aside.

In a large bowl, beat the 2 eggs, granulated sugar, and oil and vanilla until thick and smooth. In another bowl, combine the flour, the ⅔ cup cocoa, the baking soda, and salt. Stir to blend. Add the dry ingredients to the egg mixture alternately with the buttermilk or yogurt in 2 increments, and beat until smooth. Stir in the nuts. Spoon half of the chocolate mixture into the prepared pan. Carefully spoon the cheese filling over. Spoon the remaining chocolate mixture over and smooth the top.

Bake for 1 hour and 15 minutes, or until a cake tester inserted in the center comes out clean. Let cool in the pan for 15 minutes, then unmold right side up on a wire rack. Let cool completely.

In a small bowl, combine the 1 teaspoon cocoa powder and the confectioners' sugar. Dust the cake with this mixture, shaking it through a sieve. Cut the cake into slices to serve.

*Makes one 10-inch Bundt or tube cake; serves 12*

## Cheese Filling

1 cup (8 ounces) cream cheese at room temperature

¼ cup granulated sugar

1 teaspoon vanilla extract

1 large egg

1 cup (6 ounces) semisweet chocolate chips

2 large eggs

2 cups granulated sugar

1 cup canola oil

1 teaspoon vanilla extract

3 cups unbleached all-purpose flour

⅔ cup unsweetened cocoa powder, plus 1 teaspoon

2 teaspoons baking soda

½ teaspoon salt

1 cup buttermilk or low-fat plain yogurt

¾ cup (3 ounces) coarsely chopped walnuts

2 tablespoons confectioners' sugar

# mocha-cappuccino marbled coffee cake

12 tablespoons (1½ sticks) unsalted butter at room temperature

1½ cups sugar

3 large eggs

1½ teaspoons vanilla extract

2 tablespoons instant coffee powder dissolved in 2 tablespoons hot water

2½ cups unbleached all-purpose flour

1½ teaspoons baking powder

¾ teaspoon baking soda

¼ teaspoon salt

1¼ cups sour cream

2 ounces unsweetened chocolate, melted

*A swirl of chocolate* threads this coffee-flavored butter cake for a sumptuous treat with cappuccinos or lattes.

Preheat the oven to 350°F. Butter and flour a 10-inch Bundt or tube pan.

In a large bowl, cream the butter and sugar with a wooden spoon or an electric mixer until light and fluffy. Beat in the eggs, one at a time, and mix in the vanilla and dissolved coffee until blended.

In a medium bowl, combine the flour, baking powder, baking soda, and salt. Stir to blend. Add the dry ingredients to the creamed mixture alternately with the sour cream in 2 increments, beating until thick and smooth. Spoon one-third of the batter into a small bowl and stir in the chocolate. Spoon 4 heaping tablespoons of the coffee batter into the pan, spacing them apart, then spoon some chocolate batter by the table-spoon into the spaces. Repeat until all the batter is used. With a knife, swirl through the mixture once to marble the batters.

Bake for 55 minutes to 1 hour, or until a cake tester inserted in the center comes out clean. Let cool in the pan for 15 minutes, then un-mold right side up on a wire rack and let cool completely. Cut into slices to serve.

*Makes one 10-inch Bundt or tube cake; serves 12*

# blueberry-orange bundt cake

**This is an exceptional** fine-textured, moist cake, polka-dotted with juicy berries throughout. The blueberries make it healthful as well as delicious.

Preheat the oven to 325°F. Butter and flour a 10-inch Bundt or tube pan.

In a large bowl, cream the cheese and butter with a wooden spoon or an electric mixer until fluffy. Gradually add the granulated sugar and orange zest, beating until light and fluffy. Beat in the eggs, one at a time, until smooth.

In a medium bowl, combine the flour, baking powder, baking soda, and salt. Stir to blend. Add the dry ingredients to the cheese mixture alternately with the orange juice and yogurt in 2 increments, beating until thick and smooth. Stir in the blueberries. Spread the batter evenly in the pan.

Bake for 50 to 55 minutes, or until the cake is golden brown and a cake tester inserted in the center comes out clean. Let the cake cool in the pan for 15 minutes, then unmold right side up on a wire rack and let cool completely. Dust with confectioners' sugar and cut into slices to serve.

*Makes one 10-inch Bundt or tube cake; serves 12 to 16*

1 cup (8 ounces) light or regular cream cheese at room temperature

8 tablespoons (1 stick) unsalted butter at room temperature

1½ cups granulated sugar

1 tablespoon grated orange zest

5 large eggs

2⅔ cups unbleached all-purpose flour

2 teaspoons baking powder

½ teaspoon baking soda

¼ teaspoon salt

¼ cup freshly squeezed orange juice

1 cup plain yogurt

1½ cups fresh or frozen blueberries

Confectioners' sugar for dusting

# chocolate streusel—ribboned bundt cake

## Chocolate Streusel

2 tablespoons cold unsalted butter, cut into bits

3 tablespoons unbleached all-purpose flour

⅓ cup firmly packed light brown sugar

1½ teaspoons ground cinnamon

2 tablespoons unsweetened cocoa powder

¾ cup (3 ounces) chopped pecans or walnuts

8 tablespoons (1 stick) unsalted butter at room temperature

¾ cup granulated sugar

3 large eggs

1 teaspoon vanilla extract

¼ teaspoon almond extract

2 cups unbleached all-purpose flour

1 teaspoon baking powder

½ teaspoon baking soda

¼ teaspoon salt

1 cup sour cream

**In this old-time favorite,** which was popular decades ago, a cinnamon-chocolate streusel ribbons the center and tops the fine-textured cake.

Preheat the oven to 350°F. Butter and flour a 10-inch Bundt or tube pan.

To make the chocolate streusel: In a medium bowl or a food processor, combine the butter, flour, brown sugar, cinnamon, and cocoa. Cut the butter in with your fingers or process until crumbly. Stir in the nuts and set aside.

In a large bowl, cream the 8 tablespoons butter and granulated sugar with a wooden spoon or an electric mixer until light and fluffy. Add the eggs, one at a time, and the vanilla and almond extracts and beat until smooth. In a medium bowl, combine the flour, baking powder, baking soda, and salt. Stir to blend. Add the dry ingredients to the creamed mixture alternately with the sour cream in 2 increments, blending until smooth. Turn half of the batter into the prepared pan, spreading until smooth. Sprinkle with half of the streusel. Add the remaining cake batter, spread until smooth, and sprinkle evenly with the remaining streusel.

Bake for 40 minutes, or until a cake tester inserted in the center comes out clean. Let cool in the pan for 15 minutes. Unmold right side up on a wire rack and let cool completely. Cut into slices to serve.

Makes one 10-inch Bundt or tube cake; serves 12

# rosemary-lemon polenta cake

**This golden pound cake** with a polenta crunch is imbued with a hint of rosemary. Cut it into thin slices and serve as a breakfast bread or an afternoon treat, or top with raspberries and whipped cream for an inviting dessert.

Preheat the oven to 350°F. Butter and flour a 10-inch Bundt or tube pan.

In a small saucepan, combine the buttermilk and rosemary or lavender. Heat over low heat until bubbles form around the edges of the pan. Pour over the polenta or cornmeal in a small bowl; let stand for 1 hour to soften.

In a large bowl, beat the butter and sugar with a wooden spoon or an electric mixer until light and fluffy. Add the eggs, lemon zest, and vanilla and beat until blended. In a medium bowl, combine the flour, baking powder, baking soda, and salt. Stir to blend. Add the dry ingredients to the butter mixture alternately with the buttermilk mixture in 2 increments, mixing until combined. Add the batter to the prepared pan and smooth the top.

Bake for 50 minutes, or until the cake is golden brown and a cake tester inserted in the center comes out clean.

*continued*

1 cup buttermilk

2 tablespoons minced fresh rosemary or fresh lavender blossoms, or 1½ tablespoons dried lavender blossoms

½ cup finely ground polenta or cornmeal

1 cup (2 sticks) unsalted butter at room temperature

1¼ cups sugar

4 large eggs

1 tablespoon grated lemon zest

1½ teaspoons vanilla extract

2¼ cups unbleached all-purpose flour

2 teaspoons baking powder

¾ teaspoon baking soda

¼ teaspoon salt

## Rosemary-Lemon Syrup

⅓ cup sugar

⅓ cup freshly squeezed lemon juice

⅓ cup water

2 tablespoons minced fresh rosemary or fresh lavender blossoms, or 1½ tablespoons dried lavender blossoms

# *rosemary-lemon* polenta cake

CONTINUED

Meanwhile, make the rosemary-lemon syrup: In a small saucepan, combine the sugar, lemon juice, water, and rosemary or lavender. Bring to a simmer over low heat and cook for 5 minutes. Remove from the heat and stir briefly. Let cool for 30 minutes and strain through a fine-meshed sieve.

Let the cake cool in the pan for 10 minutes. Unmold right side up on a wire rack. While the cake is still warm, drizzle it with the syrup. Cut into slices to serve.

*Makes one 10-inch Bundt or tube cake; serves 16 to 20*

# holiday cranberry-nut bourbon cake

**This is a variation** on a cranberry-nut cake a renowned cookbook author and friend, Peggy Fallon, served for a holiday buffet party. It was a winner, surpassing far richer and more glamorous cakes.

Preheat the oven to 350°F. Butter and flour a 9-inch Bundt or tube pan.

In a large bowl, mix the eggs, granulated sugar, orange zest, and oil with a wooden spoon or an electric mixer until blended.

In a medium bowl, combine the flour, baking powder, and baking soda. Stir to blend. Gradually add the dry ingredients to the egg mixture alternately with the buttermilk in 2 increments. Mix just until blended. Fold in the cranberries, dates or raisins, and pecans. Pour the batter into the prepared pan, smoothing the top evenly.

Bake for 35 minutes, or until the cake is golden brown and a cake tester inserted in the center comes out with very few crumbs.

Place the pan on a wire rack. Combine the orange juice and bourbon or Scotch and pour evenly over the hot cake. Let the cake cool in the pan for 10 to 15 minutes, then carefully unmold right side up on a wire rack. Let cool completely. Dust with confectioners' sugar and cut into slices to serve.

*Makes one 9-inch Bundt or tube cake; serves 12*

2 large eggs

1 cup granulated sugar

2 tablespoons grated orange zest

¾ cup canola oil

2½ cups unbleached all-purpose flour

1 teaspoon baking powder

1 teaspoon baking soda

1 cup buttermilk

1 cup fresh or frozen cranberries

1 cup chopped pitted dates or golden raisins

1 cup (4 ounces) coarsely chopped toasted pecans

¼ cup freshly squeezed orange juice

¼ cup bourbon or Scotch whisky

Confectioners' sugar for dusting

# almond-crusted butter cake

½ cup (2 ounces) slivered or sliced
  almonds

1½ cups (3 sticks) unsalted butter
  at room temperature

1 pound powdered sugar

6 eggs

2 teaspoons vanilla extract

½ teaspoon almond extract

½ teaspoon salt

2¾ cups cake flour

**During baking, the almonds** toast, forming a buttery nut-brown coating on this fine-textured cake. Slice thinly to savor with cappuccino. This has been a favorite in my home for decades.

Preheat the oven to 300°F. Lightly butter a 10-inch Bundt or tube pan and coat the sides with the almonds.

In a large bowl, cream the butter with a wooden spoon or an electric mixer until light. Gradually add the sugar and beat until light and fluffy. Add the eggs, one at a time, and beat until smooth. Mix in the vanilla and almond extracts and the salt. Gradually add the flour, beating until smooth and fluffy. Spread the batter evenly in the prepared pan.

Bake for 1 hour and 15 to 25 minutes, or until the cake is golden brown and a cake tester inserted in the center comes out clean. Let the cake cool in the pan for 15 minutes, then unmold right side up on a wire rack to cool completely. Cut into slices to serve.

*Makes one 10-inch Bundt or tube cake; serves 16 to 20*

**LOAF VARIATION:** Prepare two 4½-by-8½-inch loaf pans as above, then add the batter, smooth the top, and bake for 1 hour, or until the loaves are golden brown and a cake tester inserted in the center comes out clean. Cut into slices to serve. Makes 2 small loaves; serves 16 to 20.

# apricot-pistachio-lemon coffee cake

**This handsome cake** makes a regal sight on a pedestal plate. Each lemon-flavored slice is colorfully flecked with pistachios and apricots. Enjoy it with a cup of Earl Grey tea or mellow Kenyan or Ethiopian coffee.

Preheat the oven to 350°F. Butter and flour a 10-inch Bundt or tube pan.

In a large bowl, cream the butter and sugar with a wooden spoon or an electric mixer until light and fluffy. Add the eggs, one at a time, beating well. Mix in the lemon zest, lemon juice, and yogurt. In a medium bowl, combine the flour, baking powder, baking soda, and salt. Stir to blend. Add the dry ingredients to the butter mixture, mixing just until blended. Stir in the apricots and nuts. Spread evenly in the prepared pan.

Bake for 50 to 55 minutes, or until the cake is golden brown and a cake tester inserted in the center comes out clean. Let the cake cool in the pan for 15 minutes, then unmold right side up on a wire rack and let cool completely. Cut into slices to serve.

*Makes one 10-inch Bundt or tube cake; serves 12 to 16*

**CHERRY-HAZELNUT VARIATION:** Follow the recipe above, substituting 1¼ cups dried cherries for the dried apricots and ¾ cup toasted and skinned hazelnuts (see note, page 47), whole or chopped, for the pistachios.

1 cup (2 sticks) unsalted butter at room temperature

1¾ cups sugar

4 large eggs

1 tablespoon grated lemon zest

2 tablespoons freshly squeezed lemon juice

1 cup plain yogurt

3 cups unbleached all-purpose flour

2 teaspoons baking powder

¾ teaspoon baking soda

¼ teaspoon salt

1¼ cups chopped dried apricots

¾ cup (3 ounces) unsalted pistachios

# lemon-glazed buttermilk bundt cake

3 large eggs

1 cup sugar

2 tablespoons grated lemon zest

¾ cup canola oil

2½ cups unbleached all-purpose flour

¼ teaspoon freshly grated or ground nutmeg

1 teaspoon baking powder

1 teaspoon baking soda

¼ teaspoon salt

1 cup buttermilk or low-fat plain yogurt

1 cup (4 ounces) coarsely chopped unsalted roasted cashew nuts or slivered almonds

## Glaze

1 tablespoon grated lemon zest

½ cup freshly squeezed lemon juice

½ cup sugar

*A tangy lemon syrup* gilds this golden cake, offsetting the sweet morsels of cashew nuts. This whips up in a jiffy and is enhanced by a side pairing of fruit: strawberries, raspberries, or fresh Bing cherries.

Preheat the oven to 350°F. Butter and flour a 9- or 10-inch Bundt or tube pan.

In a large bowl, mix the eggs, sugar, lemon zest, and oil with a wooden spoon or an electric mixer until blended.

In a medium bowl, combine the flour, nutmeg, baking powder, baking soda, and salt. Stir to blend. Gradually add the dry ingredients to the egg mixture alternately with the buttermilk or yogurt in 2 increments. Mix just until blended. Fold in the nuts. Spread the batter evenly in the prepared pan.

Bake for 35 minutes, or until the cake is golden brown and a cake tester inserted in the center comes out clean.

Meanwhile, make the glaze: In a small saucepan, combine the lemon zest, lemon juice, and sugar and heat over medium heat, stirring until the sugar is dissolved; set aside and let cool.

Let the cake cool in the pan for 10 minutes, then unmold right side up on a serving plate. Pour the syrup evenly over the warm cake. Serve at room temperature, cut into slices.

*Makes one 9- or 10-inch Bundt or tube cake; serves 12*

# orange-frosted sponge cake

*An orange-scented* confectioners' sugar frosting sheaths this delicate golden cake. Using an unbuttered tube pan helps the batter to cling to the sides.

Preheat the oven to 325°F.

In a large bowl, combine the flour, 1 cup of the sugar, the salt, and baking powder and stir to blend. In another large bowl, combine the egg whites and cream of tartar and beat with an electric mixer on high speed until soft peaks form. Gradually beat in the remaining ½ cup sugar until stiff, glossy peaks form.

Add the egg yolks, orange juice, and vanilla to the flour mixture and beat on medium speed for 1 minute, scraping down the sides of the bowl once or twice. Stir about one-fourth of the egg whites into the yolk mixture, and then fold in the remaining whites until blended. Pour the batter into an unbuttered 10-inch tube pan and smooth the top.

Bake for 50 minutes, or until the cake is golden brown, springs back when lightly touched, and a cake tester inserted in the center comes out clean. Invert on a wire rack and let cool completely. Unmold and transfer to a serving plate.

To make the orange frosting: In a medium bowl, combine all the ingredients and mix until blended. Spread over the top and sides of the cake and let set for about 1 hour. Cut into wedges to serve.

*Makes one 10-inch cake; serves 16*

1¼ cups cake flour

1½ cups sugar

½ teaspoon salt

½ teaspoon baking powder

6 large eggs, separated

1 teaspoon cream of tartar

¼ cup fresh orange juice

1 teaspoon vanilla extract

## Orange Frosting

3 tablespoons unsalted butter at room temperature

2 cups confectioners' sugar, sifted

1 tablespoon thawed frozen orange juice concentrate mixed with 2 tablespoons water

delectable
dessert cakes

**THESE SUMPTUOUS CAKES OFFER** a potpourri of fruit, nut, and chocolate flavors. In some, ground nuts serve as flour, lending both body and flavor. The baked-on toppings of fresh fruit, nuts, and chocolate wafers lend eye appeal and take the place of frosting. Any one of these beautiful cakes will make an occasion special.

# fresh pineapple–macadamia nut upside-down cake

## Fruit Layer

3 tablespoons unsalted butter

2/3 cup firmly packed light brown sugar

1 tablespoon light corn syrup

1/2 ripe pineapple, peeled, cored, and cut into 6 to 8 slices 3/8 inch thick

1/2 cup (2 ounces) unsalted macadamia nuts or cashew nuts

6 tablespoons unsalted butter at room temperature

2/3 cup granulated sugar

2 large eggs

1 teaspoon vanilla extract

1 1/2 cups cake flour

1 1/2 teaspoons baking powder

1/8 teaspoon freshly grated or ground nutmeg

1/4 teaspoon salt

3/4 cup milk

**Fresh pineapple slices** are a tart-sweet replacement for the canned pineapple rings that originally topped this upside-down cake, a cooking contest winner from the 1920s. It quickly became popular and is still an old-fashioned favorite of many people. Macadamia or cashew nuts lace the caramel-coated fruit with a sweet crunch.

Preheat the oven to 350°F.

To make the fruit layer: In a heavy 9-inch ovenproof skillet, melt the butter over medium heat. Add the brown sugar and corn syrup and cook, stirring constantly, until the sugar melts and the mixture is bubbly. Cut the pineapple slices crosswise into 3-inch pieces and immediately arrange the slices in the caramel in one layer. Place the nuts in the gaps between the pineapple slices.

In a large bowl, cream the 6 tablespoons butter and granulated sugar with a wooden spoon or an electric mixer until light and fluffy. Add the eggs, one at a time, and vanilla and beat well. In a medium bowl, combine the flour, baking powder, nutmeg, and salt. Stir to blend. Beat the dry ingredients into the creamed mixture alternately with the milk in 2 additions. Spread the batter evenly over the fruit layer.

Bake for 35 to 40 minutes, or until the cake is golden brown and a cake tester inserted in the center comes out clean. Remove from the oven and let cool in the pan for 2 minutes. Then turn upside-down onto a serving plate. Serve warm or at room temperature, cut into wedges.

Makes one 9-inch cake; serves 10

# chocolate-topped date cake

8 ounces dates, pitted and finely sliced (1⅓ cups)

1 teaspoon baking soda

¾ cup boiling water

6 tablespoons unsalted butter at room temperature

⅓ cup packed light brown sugar

½ cup granulated sugar

2 eggs

1⅔ cups unbleached all-purpose flour

1 teaspoon baking powder

¼ teaspoon salt

½ cup (3 ounces) bittersweet chocolate wafers or chocolate chips

## Topping

½ cup (3 ounces) bittersweet chocolate wafers or chocolate chips

½ cup chopped walnuts

1 tablespoon granulated sugar

1 teaspoon unsweetened cocoa powder

**Chocolate wafers and walnuts** gild the top of this moist cake forming a dazzling built-in frosting. I like to use E. Guittard 61 percent bittersweet chocolate wafers for a pretty polka-dot look and a sumptuous flavor. For a variation, try it with white or milk chocolate E. Guittard wafers.

Preheat the oven to 325°F. Butter and flour a 9-inch springform pan. Put the dates in a small bowl, sprinkle with the baking soda, and pour the boiling water over. Let stand until cooled to room temperature.

In a large bowl, cream the butter and sugars with a wooden spoon or an electric mixer until light and fluffy. Add the eggs and beat until smooth. In a small bowl, combine the flour, baking powder, and salt. Stir to blend. Beat the flour mixture into the creamed mixture alternately with the date and water mixture in two increments, mixing until blended. Stir in the ½ cup chocolate wafers or chips.

Turn the batter into the prepared pan and spread evenly. For the topping, scatter the chocolate wafers or chips evenly over the batter. Toss the nuts with the 1 tablespoon granulated sugar and the cocoa and sprinkle evenly over the chocolate.

Bake for 40 to 45 minutes, or until the cake is set and a cake tester inserted in the center comes out moist. Let cool in the pan on a wire rack for 30 minutes before removing the sides. Cut into wedges to serve.

**Makes one 9-inch cake; serves 12**

**NOTE:** E. Guittard chocolate wafers are available in specialty foods shops and online at eguittard.com.

# chocolate-almond soufflé cake

Chocolate shreds fleck this luscious nut soufflé cake for an elegant treat with your favorite brew: Mocha-Java, Kona, or Ethiopian, perhaps. Or go all out pairing the slices with rich hot chocolate topped with whipped cream. Use a premium chocolate such as Guittard or Sharffen Berger to accent the delicate cake with an intense bittersweet flavor.

. . . . . . . . . . . . . . . . . . . . . . . . . . . .

Preheat the oven to 350°F. Butter and flour a 9-inch springform pan.

Scatter the nuts on a baking sheet and bake for 8 to 10 minutes or until lightly toasted. Let cool. Using a food processor or blender, process the chocolate until finely grated. Turn out into a bowl. Process the nuts until finely ground and add to the chocolate.

In a large bowl, beat the egg whites until foamy, add the salt and cream of tartar, and beat until soft peaks form. Add the 2 tablespoons brown sugar and beat until stiff, glossy peaks form. In a medium bowl, beat the egg yolks until thick and pale in color. Beat in the 1 cup brown sugar and the vanilla and almond extracts until thick and pale in color. Stir the flour into the nut and chocolate mixture and fold half of it into the yolk mixture. Fold one-third of the whites in to lighten it. Fold in the remaining nut and chocolate mixture, then gently fold in the remaining whites. Spread evenly in the prepared pan.

Bake for 30 to 35 minutes, or until the top springs back when touched lightly. Let cool completely in the pan on a wire rack. Remove the sides of the pan and cut the cake into slices to serve.

Makes one 9-inch cake; serves 10 to 12

1 1/3 cups (5 1/2 ounces) slivered or raw whole almonds

4 ounces bittersweet or semisweet chocolate

6 large eggs, separated

1/8 teaspoon salt

1/8 teaspoon cream of tartar

2 tablespoons plus 1 cup firmly packed light brown sugar

1 teaspoon vanilla extract

1/4 teaspoon almond extract

1/2 cup unbleached all-purpose flour, or 1/4 cup unbleached all-purpose flour and 1/4 cup almond meal (see note, page 117)

# marionberry-hazelnut cake

This tender nut cake delights the palate with a juicy burst of berries in each biteful. Partner with a scoop of vanilla bean ice cream or whipped cream flavored with framboise for a deluxe sweet.

Preheat the oven to 325°F. Butter and flour a 9-inch springform pan. Scatter the nut meal on a baking sheet and bake for 8 minutes, or until lightly toasted. Let cool. Increase the oven temperature to 350°F.

In a large bowl, cream the butter and sugars with a wooden spoon or an electric mixer until light and fluffy. Add the eggs, one at a time, and almond extract and beat until smooth.

In a medium bowl, combine the toasted nut meal, flour, baking powder, and 1 teaspoon of the cinnamon. Stir to blend. Gradually add the dry ingredients to the creamed mixture and beat until smooth. Spread the batter evenly in the prepared pan. Scatter the berries evenly over the top. Toss the remaining 1 teaspoon cinnamon with the Demerara or turbinado sugar and nuts and sprinkle evenly over the top.

Bake for 35 to 40 minutes, or until the cake is set when pressed lightly and a cake tester inserted in the center comes out clean. Let cool in the pan on a wire rack for 10 minutes, then remove the pan sides. Serve warm or at room temperature, cut into wedges.

Makes one 9-inch cake; serves 10 to 12

NOTE: Hazelnut and almond meal, or flour, is available in specialty food stores, or you can grind the nuts finely in a food processor (hazelnuts should be toasted and skinned first; see page 47).

1¼ cups ground hazelnut meal or almond meal (see note)

8 tablespoons (1 stick) unsalted butter at room temperature

½ cup granulated sugar

½ cup firmly packed light brown sugar

3 large eggs

½ teaspoon almond extract

½ cup unbleached all-purpose flour

1½ teaspoons baking powder

2 teaspoons ground cinnamon

2 cups fresh or frozen marionberries or mixed blackberries, raspberries, and blueberries

2 tablespoons Demerara or turbinado sugar

⅓ cup hazelnuts, toasted, skinned, and chopped (see note, page 47), or sliced or slivered almonds

# prize navel orange and almond cake

2 large navel oranges, scrubbed

1½ cups (6 ounces) slivered almonds

2 tablespoons unbleached
all-purpose flour

6 large eggs

1 cup sugar

¼ teaspoon salt

1 teaspoon baking powder

Navel oranges perfume this ultra-moist cake. The recipe is unusual as the oranges are simmered in water until very soft, then ground, peel and all. Sometimes I use half hazelnuts and half almonds. A local celebrity gave me the recipe decades ago, and I later discovered it was a favorite of James Beard.

Preheat the oven to 400°F. Butter and flour a 9-inch springform pan.

Put the unpeeled oranges in a large saucepan and add water to cover. Cover the pan and bring to a boil over medium heat. Reduce the heat to a simmer and cook until very soft, about 40 minutes.

Meanwhile, process the almonds and flour in a food processor until finely ground. Transfer to a medium bowl.

Drain, cool, and cut the oranges into quarters, removing any seeds. In the food processor, process the oranges to make a lightly textured purée.

In a large bowl, beat the eggs until thick and pale in color. Gradually beat in the sugar until smooth. Add the purée to the egg mixture. Add the salt and baking powder to the almond mixture and stir to blend. Stir the dry ingredients into the egg mixture until blended. Turn into the prepared pan and smooth the top.

Bake for 1 hour, or until the cake is set when pressed lightly. Place the pan on a wire rack and let cool completely. Remove the pan sides and unmold right side up on a serving plate. Cut into wedges to serve.

Makes one 9-inch cake; serves 10

# ginger-trio gingerbread

**With a combination** of fresh, ground, and crystallized ginger, this cake exudes a zingy hot spiciness for a perfect match with cappuccino or Mocha-Java or Viennese-roast coffee.

. . . . . . . . . . . . . . . . . . . . . . . . . . . . . . . . . . . . . . . . . .

Preheat the oven to 375°F. Lightly butter and flour a 9-inch springform pan that is 2 inches deep.

In a large bowl, cream the butter, fresh ginger, honey, and molasses with a wooden spoon or an electric mixer until blended. Add the yogurt and eggs, one at a time, mixing until smooth.

In a medium bowl, combine the flour, baking soda, salt, ground ginger, mustard, allspice, and cinnamon. Stir well to blend. Add the dry ingredients to the butter mixture and mix until blended. Spread evenly in the prepared pan and sprinkle evenly with the crystallized ginger.

Bake for 30 to 35 minutes, or until the cake is set when pressed lightly and a cake tester inserted in the center comes out clean. Let the cake cool in the pan on a wire rack for 5 minutes, then remove the pan sides. Serve warm or at room temperature, cut into wedges and topped with whipped cream or frozen yogurt, if desired.

*Makes one 9-inch cake; serves 10 to 12*

8 tablespoons (1 stick) unsalted butter, melted

3 tablespoons grated or finely chopped peeled fresh ginger

1/2 cup honey

1/2 cup dark molasses

1/2 cup plain yogurt

2 large eggs

2 cups unbleached all-purpose flour

1 1/2 teaspoons baking soda

1/4 teaspoon salt

1/2 teaspoon ground ginger

1/2 teaspoon dry mustard

1/2 teaspoon ground allspice

1/2 teaspoon ground cinnamon

1/2 cup chopped crystallized ginger

Whipped cream or frozen yogurt for serving (optional)

# essence of orange–chocolate wafer cake

**This ranks among** my top favorite cakes. Diminutive chocolate wafers form a festive polka-dot pattern on this tender golden cake. Their bittersweet flavor is a seductive counterbalance to the vibrant tang of orange zest. Serve it slightly warm so the chocolate oozes with melting goodness. A whole orange, including the peel, and golden raisins lend a long-lasting moistness to the cake.

Preheat the oven to 350°F. Butter and flour a 10-inch springform pan or 9-inch square pan.

Remove a thin slice from the stem end of the orange and cut the fruit into eighths, leaving the peel on. In a food processor, combine the orange segments and raisins and process until finely ground.

In a large bowl, cream the butter and sugar with a wooden spoon or an electric mixer until light and fluffy. Add the eggs, one at a time, beating well. Mix in the orange mixture. In a medium bowl, combine the flour, baking powder, baking soda, and salt. Stir to blend. Add the dry ingredients to the creamed mixture alternately with the yogurt or buttermilk in 2 increments, beating until blended. Reserve ¼ cup of the chocolate for the topping and mix the remainder into the batter. Spread evenly in the prepared pan. Sprinkle the reserved chocolate evenly over the top.

*continued*

1 large orange, scrubbed

1 cup golden raisins

8 tablespoons (1 stick) unsalted butter at room temperature

1 cup sugar

2 large eggs

2 ¼ cups unbleached all-purpose flour

1 teaspoon baking powder

1 teaspoon baking soda

½ teaspoon salt

1 cup low-fat plain yogurt or buttermilk

1 cup (6 ounces) bittersweet chocolate wafers (see note, page 114) or chocolate chips

# essence of orange–chocolate wafer cake

CONTINUED

Bake for 35 to 40 minutes, or until the cake is golden brown and a cake tester inserted in the center comes out clean. Let cool in the pan on a wire rack for 15 minutes, then remove the pan sides. Serve slightly warm or at room temperature, cut into wedges.

Makes one 10-inch cake; serves 10 to 12

# french prune plum cake

**This was a sweet discovery** at a charming French country hotel, the L'Ancienne Boulangerie, in the hamlet of Caunes-Minervois near Carcassonne. Former Californians Terry and Lois Link had restored a former bakery into an intimate bed-and-breakfast inn there. This cake is a perfect mid-afternoon snack with a *boule* of coffee, or serve it as a dessert. The Italian prune plum has an amber interior and rich flavor. It keeps its shape during baking.

Preheat the oven to 350°F. Butter and flour a 9-inch springform pan.

In a bowl, cream the butter and sugar with a wooden spoon or an electric mixer until light and fluffy. Add the eggs, one at a time, and vanilla and beat until smooth.

In a medium bowl, combine the flour, baking powder, and salt. Stir to blend. Add the dry ingredients to the butter mixture and beat until smooth. Turn into the prepared pan and top with the plums, pressing them gently into the batter, cut side up. For the topping, drizzle the plums with the lemon juice and sprinkle with the cinnamon mixture.

Bake for 55 minutes to 1 hour, or until the cake is golden brown. Let cool in the pan on a wire rack for 10 minutes, then remove the pan sides. Serve warm or at room temperature, cut into wedges, with whipped cream or crème fraîche, if desired.

*Makes one 9-inch cake; serves 10*

8 tablespoons (1 stick) unsalted butter at room temperature

1 cup sugar

2 eggs

1 teaspoon vanilla extract

1 cup unbleached all-purpose flour

1 teaspoon baking powder

¼ teaspoon salt

12 Italian prune plums, halved and pitted

## Topping

2 tablespoons freshly squeezed lemon juice

3 tablespoons sugar mixed with 1 teaspoon ground cinnamon

Whipped cream or crème fraîche for serving (optional)

# pear pinwheel and hazelnut cake

1 cup (4 ounces) hazelnuts or
blanched almonds

2 tablespoons unbleached all-
purpose flour

8 tablespoons (1 stick) unsalted
butter at room temperature

½ cup firmly packed light brown
sugar

2 large eggs

¼ teaspoon almond extract

3 large ripe Anjou or Bosc pears,
peeled, halved, and cored

2 tablespoons confectioners' sugar

¼ teaspoon freshly grated or ground
nutmeg

1 teaspoon ground cinnamon

*Juicy sweet pears* form a pinwheel on this elegant ground-nut cake. A dusting of cinnamon-sugar makes a spicy finish.

Preheat the oven to 350°F. Butter and flour a 9-inch springform pan.

Scatter the nuts on a baking sheet and bake for 8 to 10 minutes, or until lightly toasted. If using hazelnuts, wrap them in a tea towel and rub to remove the skins. In a food processor, combine the nuts and flour and process until finely ground.

In a large bowl, cream the butter and brown sugar with a wooden spoon or an electric mixer until light and fluffy. Add the eggs, one at a time, and almond extract and beat until smooth. Mix in the nut mixture. Spread the batter in the prepared pan. Cut the pears into slices ⅜ inch thick and place in a bowl. In a small bowl, combine the confectioners' sugar, nutmeg, and cinnamon. Stir to blend. Sprinkle the fruit with the confectioners' sugar mixture, toss to coat, and arrange in a pinwheel on top of the batter.

Bake for 30 to 35 minutes, or until the cake is golden brown and a cake tester inserted in the center comes out clean. Place the pan on a wire rack and let the cake cool completely. Remove the sides of the pan and cut the cake into wedges to serve.

*Makes one 9-inch cake; serves 8 to 10*

# dark chocolate–almond cake

**This elegant chocolate** cake is my favorite for a special occasion. It needs no frosting and is sublime with a scoop or two of homemade raspberry sorbet or a Grand Marnier or vanilla bean ice cream. It is important to not overbake it; the very center should still be gently soft when at room temperature.

- - - - - - - - - - - - - - - - - - - - - - - - - - - - - - - - -

Preheat the oven to 350°F. Butter and flour a 9-inch springform pan.

In a double boiler over barely simmering water, melt the butter and chocolate and stir to blend. Let cool.

In a large bowl, beat the egg whites until foamy with a whisk or an electric mixer; add the salt and cream of tartar and beat until soft peaks form. Add the ¼ cup granulated sugar and beat until stiff, glossy peaks form.

In a medium bowl, beat the egg yolks until thick and lemon-colored, then beat in the ½ cup granulated sugar and the coffee or spirits. Stir in the chocolate mixture until blended. Fold in one-third of the whites to lighten the mixture, then fold in the nuts, flour, and then the remaining whites. Pour the batter into the prepared pan and smooth the top.

Bake for 35 minutes, or until a cake tester inserted 1½ inches from the center comes out clean (the center should still be soft). Let the cake cool completely in the pan on a wire rack before removing the pan sides.

Dust the cake with confectioners' sugar shaken through a sieve, and cut into wedges to serve.

*Makes one 9-inch cake; serves 12*

8 tablespoons (1 stick) unsalted butter

8 ounces bittersweet or semisweet chocolate, chopped

6 large eggs, separated

⅛ teaspoon salt

⅛ teaspoon cream of tartar

¼ cup granulated sugar, plus ½ cup

2 tablespoons brewed coffee, Grand Marnier, Triple Sec, or rum

¾ cup (3 ounces) finely ground almonds or toasted and skinned hazelnuts (see note, page 47)

6 tablespoons unbleached all-purpose flour

Confectioners' sugar for dusting

# chocolate-glazed raspberry-almond cake

8 ounces almond paste

6 large eggs, separated

½ cup sugar

1½ tablespoons fresh lemon juice

1 teaspoon grated lemon zest

½ cup unbleached all-purpose flour

¾ teaspoon baking powder

⅔ cup raspberry jelly

6 ounces bittersweet or semisweet
   chocolate, chopped

3 tablespoons unsalted butter

3 tablespoons sliced almonds

**This is a sumptuous** party cake to reign at a special occasion alongside richly brewed coffee. Almond paste, raspberry jelly, and dark chocolate intertwine for a showpiece dessert.

Preheat the oven to 350°F. Lightly butter and flour two 9-inch round cake pans.

Put the almond paste in a large bowl and beat in the egg yolks, one at a time, with an electric mixer until smooth. Beat in ¼ cup of the sugar, the lemon juice, and zest. In a large bowl, beat the egg whites with an electric mixer until soft peaks form, then gradually beat in the remaining ¼ cup sugar until stiff, glossy peaks form. Fold one-third of the egg whites into the yolk mixture to lighten it, then gently fold in the remaining whites. In a medium bowl, combine the flour and baking powder and stir to blend. Sprinkle the dry ingredients over the egg mixture and gently fold in. Divide the batter between the prepared pans and smooth the tops.

Bake for 30 to 35 minutes, or until the cake is golden brown and a cake tester inserted in the center comes out clean. Let the cakes cool in the pans for 5 minutes, then unmold onto wire racks and let cool completely.

To assemble, place 1 layer on a serving plate, upside down. In a small saucepan, heat the raspberry jelly until melted and spread over the cake layer; top with the remaining layer, upside down.

In a double boiler over barely simmering water, melt the chocolate and butter, stirring to blend. With a spatula, spread the chocolate glaze over the top and sides of the cake. Sprinkle the almonds around the outer edge of the top. Refrigerate for 1 hour to set the glaze. Cut into wedges to serve.

*Makes one 9-inch layer cake; serves 12*

# index

# table of equivalents

The exact equivalents in the following tables have been rounded for convenience.

## LIQUID/DRY MEASURES

| U.S. | Metric |
|---|---|
| ¼ teaspoon | 1.25 milliliters |
| ½ teaspoon | 2.5 milliliters |
| 1 teaspoon | 5 milliliters |
| 1 tablespoon (3 teaspoons) | 15 milliliters |
| 1 fluid ounce (2 tablespoons) | 30 milliliters |
| ¼ cup | 60 milliliters |
| ⅓ cup | 80 milliliters |
| ½ cup | 120 milliliters |
| 1 cup | 240 milliliters |
| 1 pint (2 cups) | 480 milliliters |
| 1 quart (4 cups; 32 ounces) | 960 milliliters |
| 1 gallon (4 quarts) | 3.84 liters |
| 1 ounce (by weight) | 28 grams |
| 1 pound | 454 grams |
| 2.2 pounds | 1 kilogram |

## LENGTH

| U.S. | Metric |
|---|---|
| ⅛ inch | 3 millimeters |
| ¼ inch | 6 millimeters |
| ½ inch | 12 millimeters |
| 1 inch | 2.5 centimeters |

## OVEN TEMPERATURE

| Fahrenheit | Celsius | Gas |
|---|---|---|
| 250 | 120 | ½ |
| 275 | 140 | 1 |
| 300 | 150 | 2 |
| 325 | 160 | 3 |
| 350 | 180 | 4 |
| 375 | 190 | 5 |
| 400 | 200 | 6 |
| 425 | 220 | 7 |
| 450 | 230 | 8 |
| 475 | 240 | 9 |
| 500 | 260 | 10 |